Conquering Pre-Kindergarten

Reading
Mathematics
Science
Social Studies
Writing

Certificate of Achievement

Contributing Authors

Reha M. Jain, Emily R. Smith, and Lynette Ordoñez

Publishing Credits

Corinne Burton, M.A.Ed., *President*; Conni Medina, M.A.Ed., *Managing Editor*; Emily R. Smith, M.A.Ed., *Content Director*; Lynette Ordoñez, *Editor*; Evan Ferrell, *Graphic Designer*; Lubabah Memon, *Assistant Editor*

Image Credits

pp. 125, 138, 145, 149, 154 Illustrations by Timothy J. Bradley; p. 134 Illustration by Evan Ferrell; all other images from iStock and/or Shutterstock.

Standards

Shell Education
A division of Teacher Created Materials
5301 Oceanus Drive
Huntington Beach, CA 92649-1030

www.tcmpub.com/shell-education
ISBN 978-1-4258-1714-5

Table of Contents

Dear Family,

Welcome to *Conquering Pre-Kindergarten*. This year will be an exciting and challenging year for your child. This book is designed to supplement the pre-kindergarten concepts your child is learning. The activities in this book are based on today's standards and provide practice in letters, numbers, shapes, writing, colors, social studies, and science. It also features fun, yet challenging, critical-thinking activities. In addition to the activity sheets in this book, the end of each section also provides engaging extension activities.

Your child should complete one unit per month, including the extension activities. This will allow your child to think about learning concepts over a longer period of time.

Keep these tips in mind as you work with your child this year:

- Set aside specific times each week to work on the activities.
- Have your child complete one or two activities each time, rather than an entire unit at one time.
- Keep all practice sessions with your child positive and constructive. If the mood becomes tense or you and your child get frustrated, set the book aside and find another time to practice.
- Read the directions aloud to your child. Point out any examples. Then, work through the first problem on each page together.
- Encourage your child to do his or her best work and compliment the effort that goes into learning.

Enjoy the time learning with your child during pre-kindergarten. Summer will be here before you know it!

Sincerely,

The Shell Education Staff

Suggested Family Activities

Extend your child's learning by taking fun family field trips. A wide variety of experiences helps develop a child's vocabulary. Field trips also provide greater context and meaning to his or her learning.

A Trip to a Museum

Your first stop should be the gift shop. Have your child pick out three postcards of artifacts or paintings in the museum. Then, as you visit the museum, your child should be on the lookout for the items he or she chose. It's an individual scavenger hunt! (Postcards usually have a bit of information about the pictured item to help you find it.)

A Trip to a National Park

The National Park Service has a great program called Junior Rangers. If you go to a national park, check in with the rangers at the visitors center to see what tasks your child can complete to earn a Junior Ranger patch and/or certificate. Your child can also go to the WebRangers site (www.nps.gov/webrangers/) and check out a vacation spot, play games, and earn virtual rewards!

A Trip to a Zoo

Before your trip, create a Zoo Bingo card. Include pictures of a variety of animals you will see at the zoo. Bring the Zoo Bingo card with you. As you spend the day exploring, have your child cross out each animal you come across. When he or she gets bingo, celebrate the accomplishment!

A Trip to a Library

Have your child pick out books he or she has never read (or that you have never read to him or her). Look carefully at the covers of the books together. Ask your child what he or she thinks the stories are going to be about based on the covers alone. Then, read the books aloud to your child, and see if his or her guess was correct.

A Trip to a Farmers' Market

Farmers' markets are great places to learn about different fruits and vegetables. Ask your child to help you find the colors of the rainbow. At each fruit or vegetable stand, ask your child to locate one color from the rainbow. Then, explain what the fruit or vegetable is and the different types of recipes it can be used in. For example, a red tomato can be used for salads, pizza, or pasta sauce.

Suggested Family Activities (cont.)

By discussing the activities in this book, you can enhance your child's learning. But it doesn't have to stop there. The suggestions below provide even more ideas on how to support your child's education.

General Skills

- Make sure your child gets plenty of exercise. Children need about 60 minutes of physical activity each day. You may want to have your child sign up for a sport. Or, you can do fun things as a family, such as swimming, riding bicycles, or hiking.
- It's also important for children to get plenty of sleep. Establish a nightly bedtime routine that involves relaxing activities, such as a warm shower or bath or reading a story.

Reading Skills

- Create an alphabet book with your child. Go through old magazines, newspapers, advertisements, etc., to find an image for each letter of the alphabet. Help your child cut out the images and glue them into a book.
- Set a reading time for the entire family at least every other day. Have your child point out letters he or she knows as you read aloud.

Writing Skills

- Have your child practice writing letters through sensory activities. For example, you could pour an impressionable substance (this could be salt, flour, sugar, pudding, shaving cream, etc.) into a cookie tray, and let your child get messy while learning to write letters.
- Supply your child with writing tools that better fit his or her hands to help develop his or her fine motor skills. Normal-length pencils are often too large and are awkward for smaller hands to hold. Golf pencils, broken crayons, and small markers will make writing more comfortable.

Mathematics Skills

- Help your child practice counting, whenever possible. You can do this in everyday situations such as counting the number of stairs, silverware pieces at the dinner table, etc.
- Involve your child in grocery shopping. Ask him or her to help solve basic mathematical problems. For example, "I have two apples in my hands. You have two apples in yours. How many apples do we have altogether?"

Directions: Trace the lines in preparation for forming letters.

Directions: Trace the lines and shapes in preparation for forming letters.

Directions: Trace the lines in preparation for forming letters.

Directions: Trace from left to right using "rainbow tracing." Use different color crayons to trace over the lines. Then, color the pictures.

Directions: Say the name of each animal. Listen as you say the beginning sound.

Directions: Draw a picture that shows you. Then, write your name.

Directions: Trace.

Directions: Write the number 1.

Directions: Say and trace.

I see ____ bird.

Directions: Trace the circles. Color the circles different colors.

Directions: Count the animals in each box. Draw lines to match the boxes that have the same number of animals.

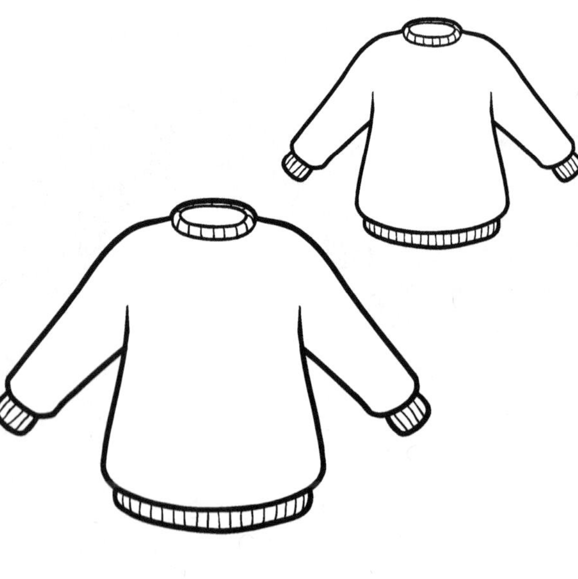

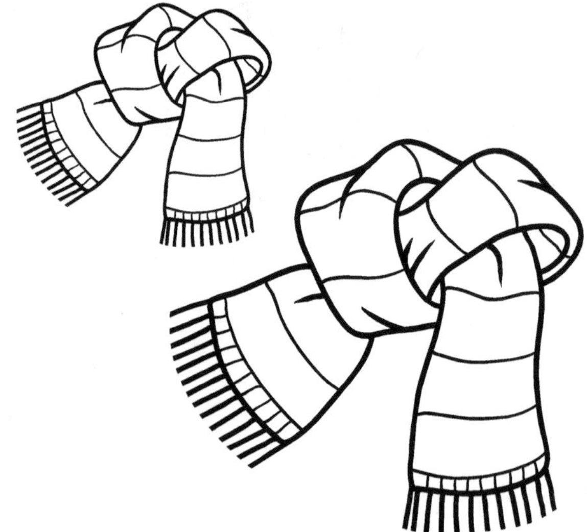

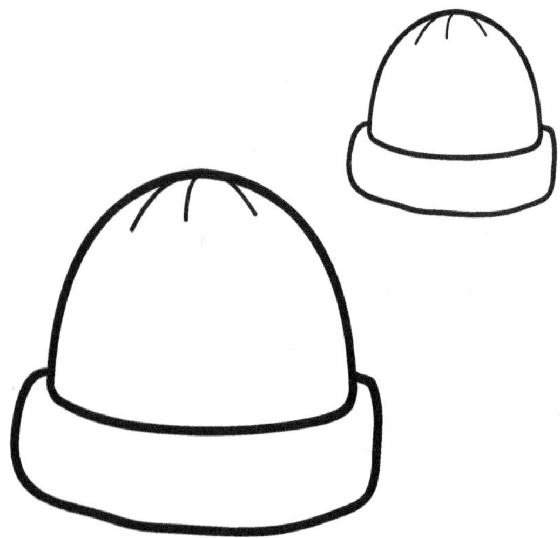

Directions: Color the larger object in each box.

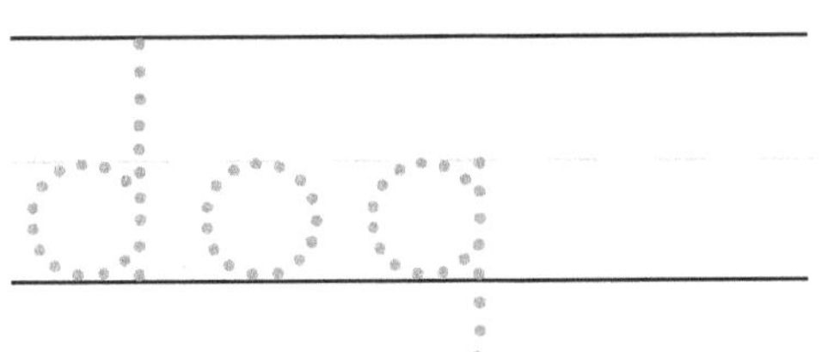

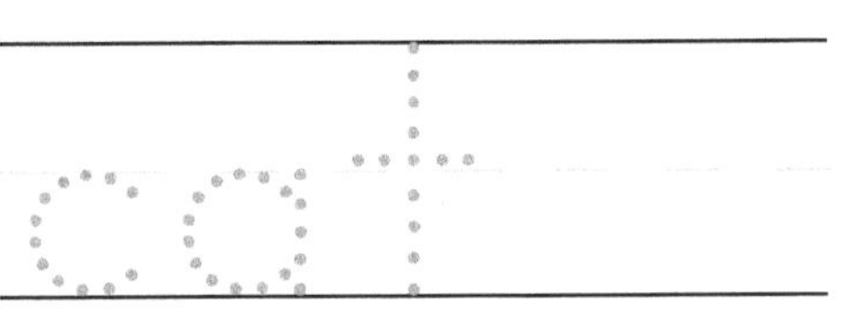

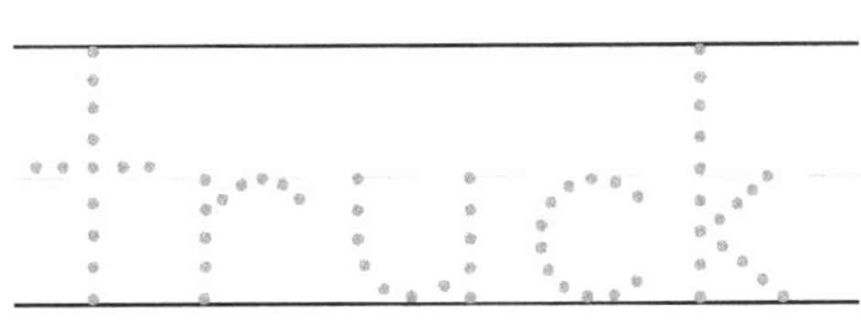

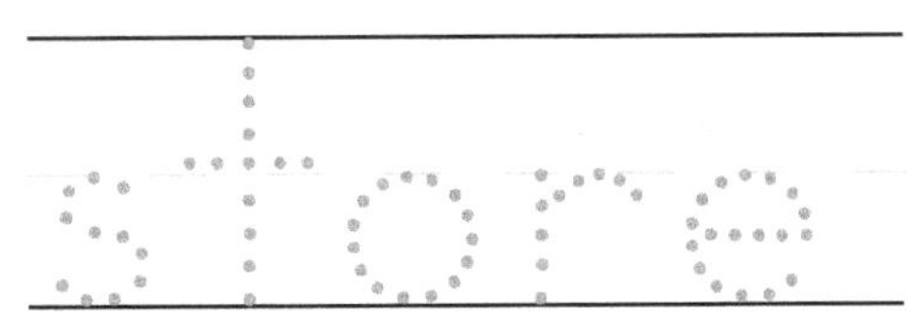

Directions: Trace each word and say it. Then, take a walk with an adult. Count how many times you see each thing in your neighborhood.

Picture Bank

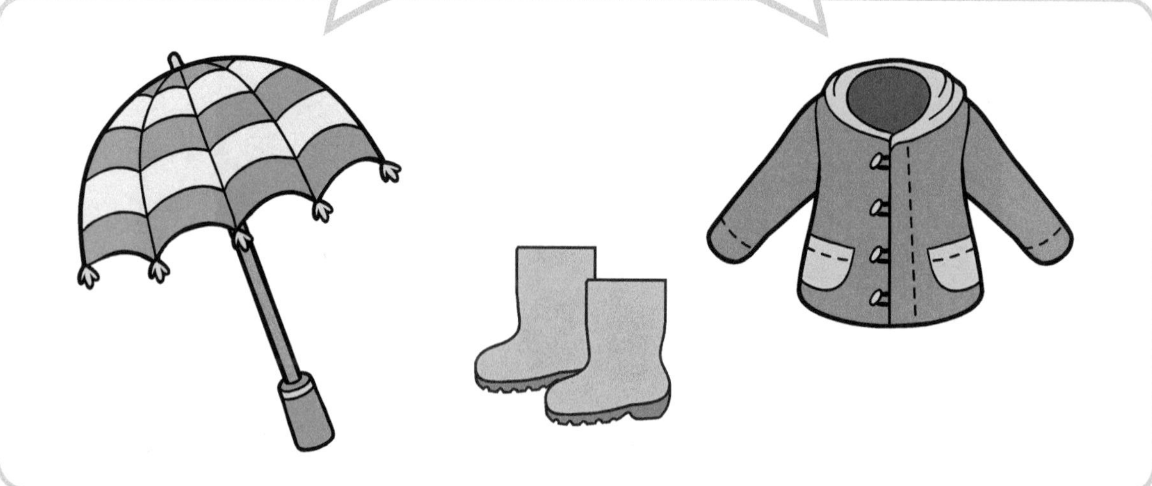

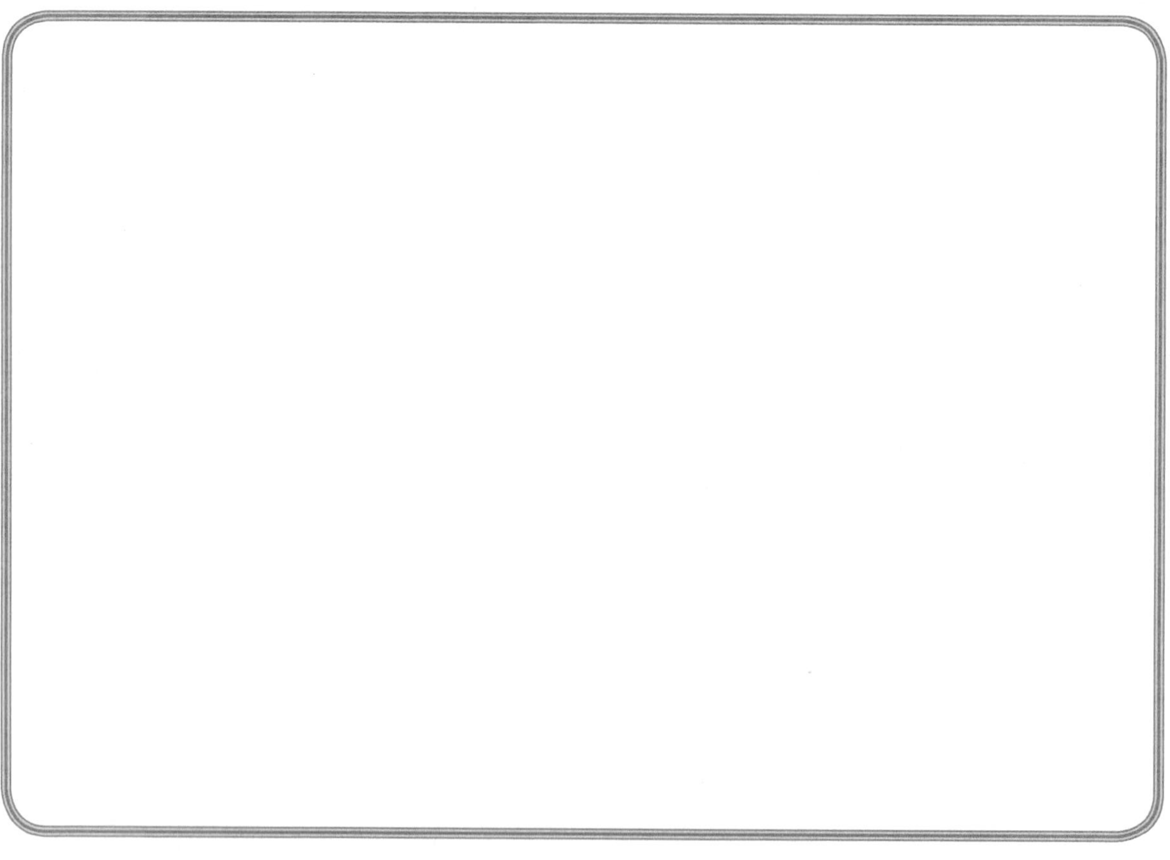

rain

Directions: Draw a picture of a person in the rain. Use all three pictures from the Picture Bank in your drawing. Then, trace the word *rain*.

Directions: Number the pictures in order. Color the pictures.

Directions: Name all the objects on the page. Use red to color anything that is red in the real world.

Language Arts Activity

Give your child a sheet of paper. Have your child use the lines he or she drew on pages 7–9 to make a picture of a place, such as a playground. Then, have your child draw himself or herself in the picture. Have your child write his or her name on the page.

Mathematics Activity

Give your child an oversized sheet of paper, such as butcher paper. Have your child draw the biggest circle possible on the paper. Then, have him or her fill the big circle with as many smaller circles as can fit. Help your child count the smaller circles. Have your child repeat the activity, this time trying to fit even more circles into the larger one.

Social Studies Activity

Ask your child to retell the events of your walk in your neighborhood. Ask him or her where you went and what you saw. Then, have your child draw a picture of himself or herself on the walk.

Critical-Thinking Activity

Have your child draw himself or herself as a baby and then as a toddler. Finally, have your child draw himself or herself as a four year old. Ask your child to describe how he or she has changed since being a baby and how your child thinks he or she will change in the years to come.

Listening-and-Speaking Activity

Ask your child to make up a story about Red Day! On Red Day, people can only wear red and eat red foods. Everything people do has to be about the color red! Ask your child to tell you his or her story.

ABC

Letters

Directions: Trace.

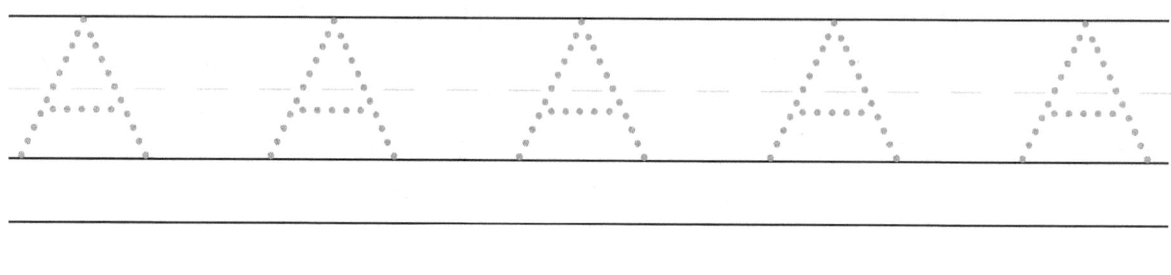

Directions: Write the letter Aa.

Directions: Say and trace.

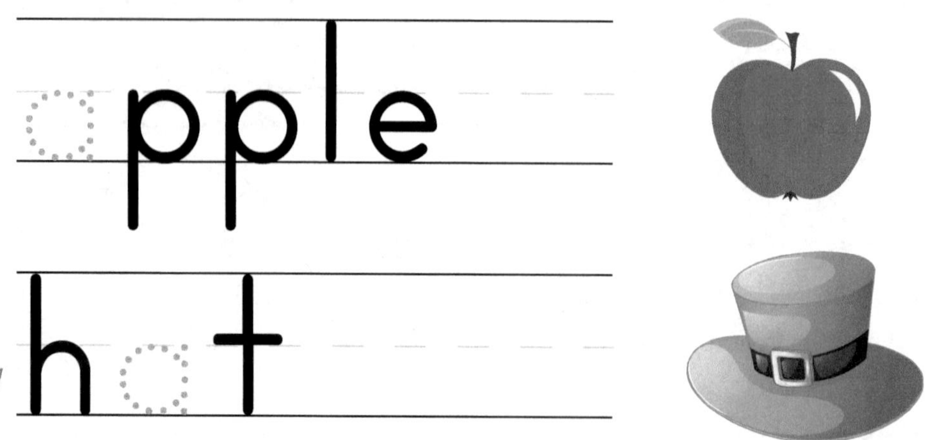

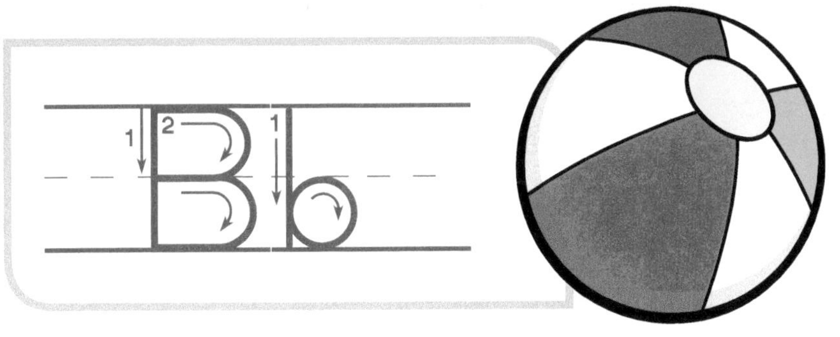

Directions: Trace.

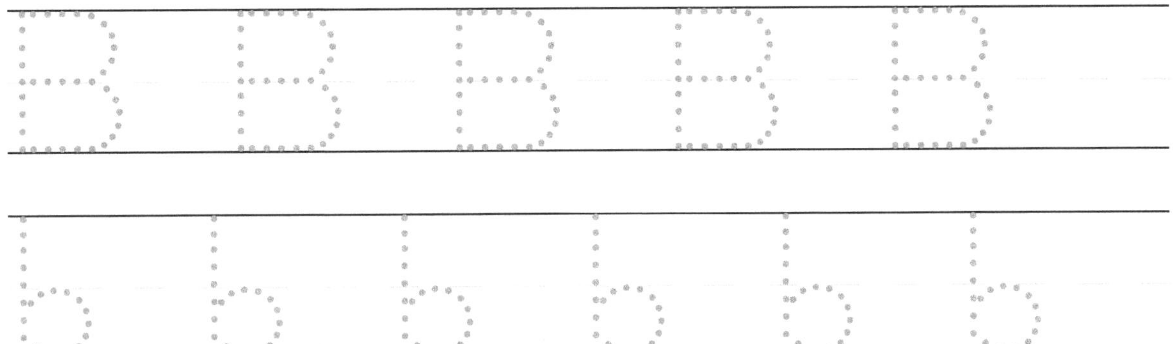

Directions: Write the letter Bb.

Directions: Say and trace.

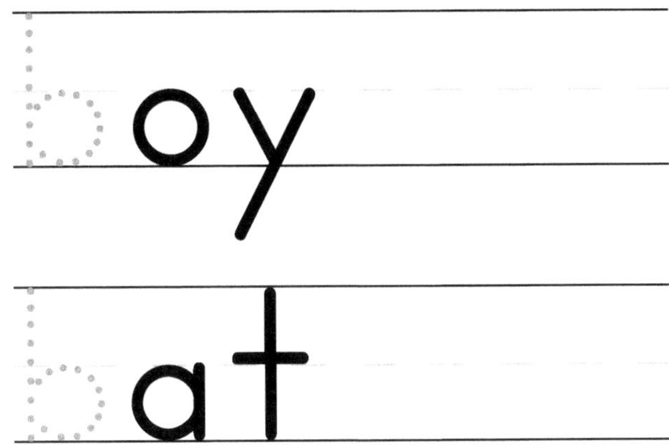

Directions: Trace.

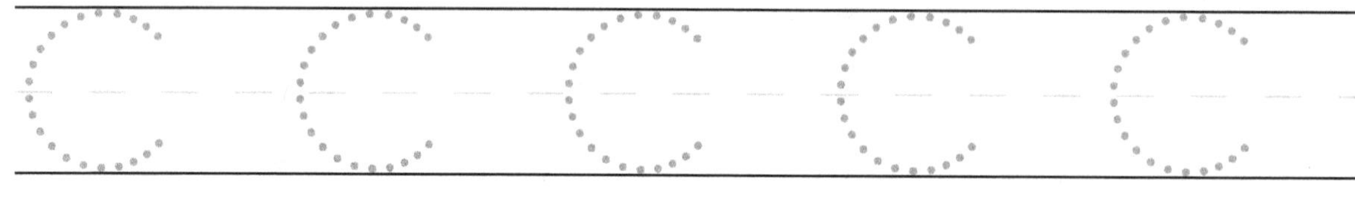

Directions: Write the letter Cc.

Directions: Say and trace.

ar

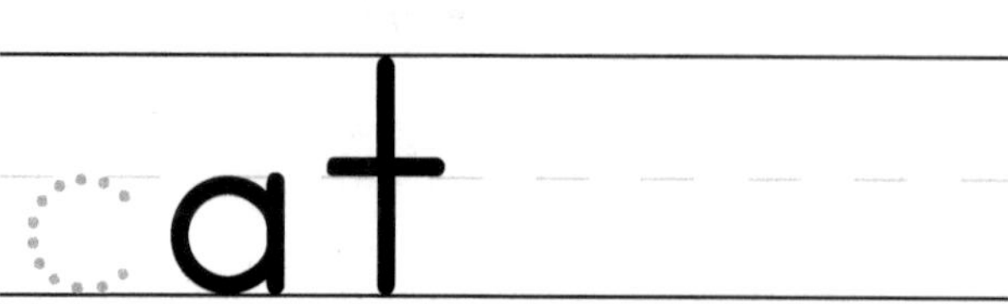

Directions: Circle all the lowercase *a*s.

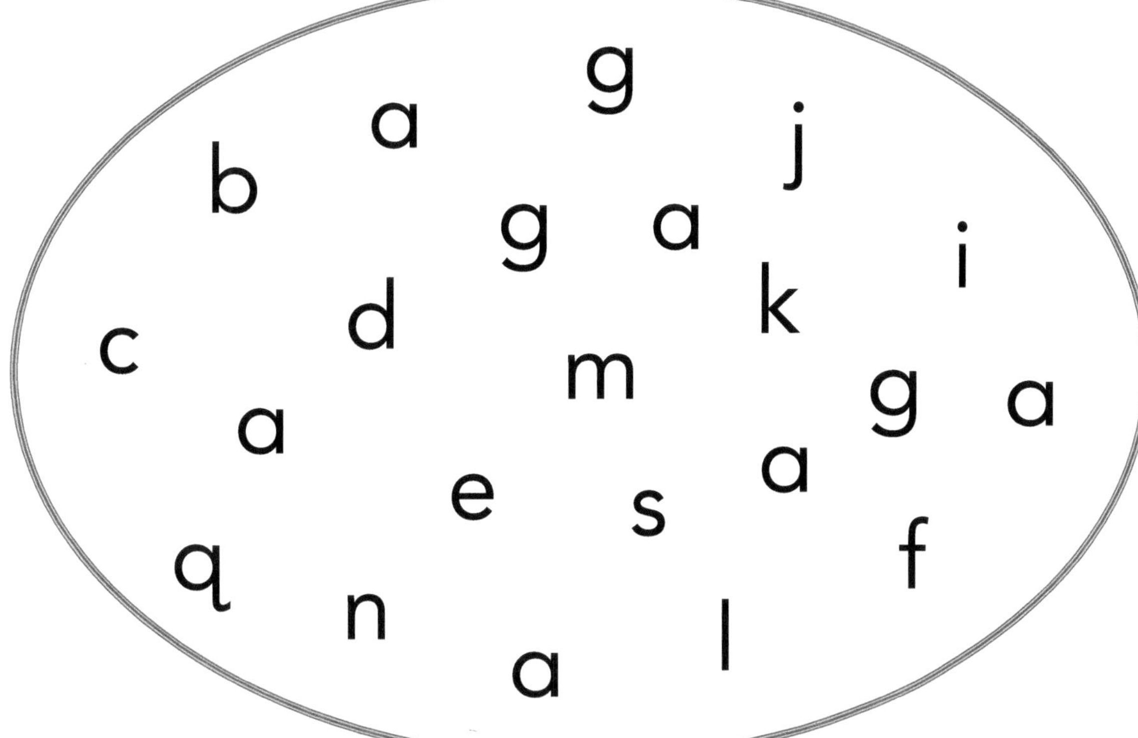

Directions: Circle all the lowercase *b*s.

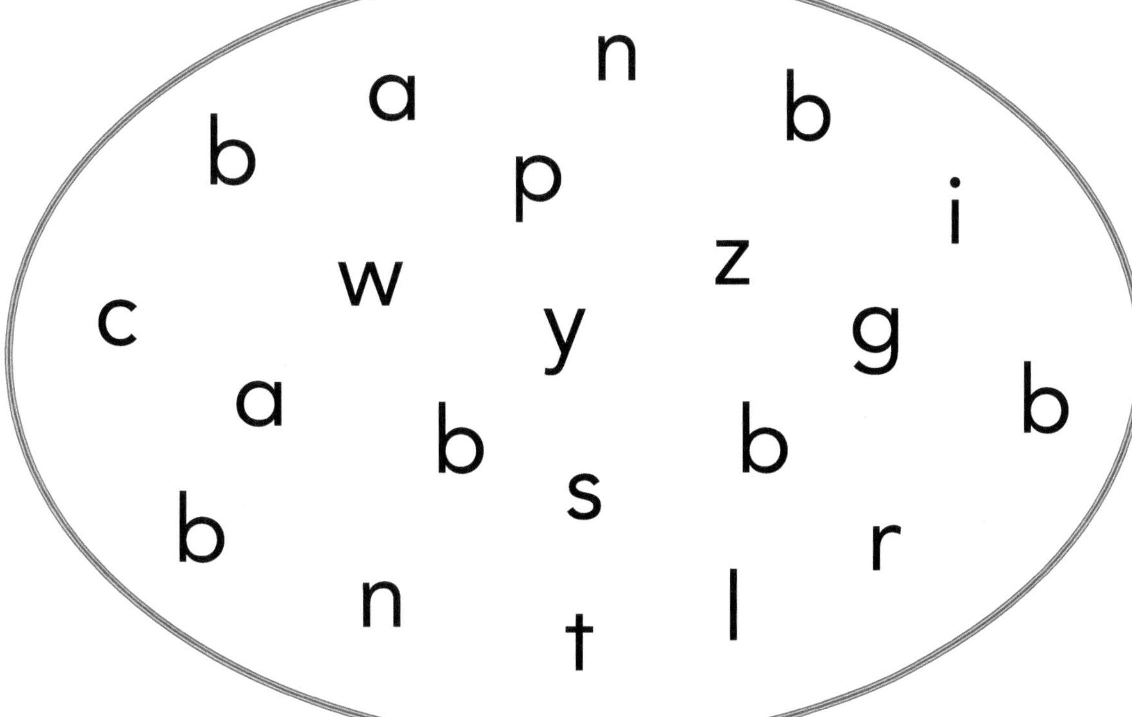

B

Directions: Say the letters on the left. Name the pictures on the right. Draw a line from each letter to the picture that begins with that letter's sound. Then, color the pictures.

Directions: Draw a picture of your family. Then, write your last name.

Directions: Trace.

2 2 2 2 2

Directions: Write the number 2.

2

Directions: Say and trace.

I see 2 cars.

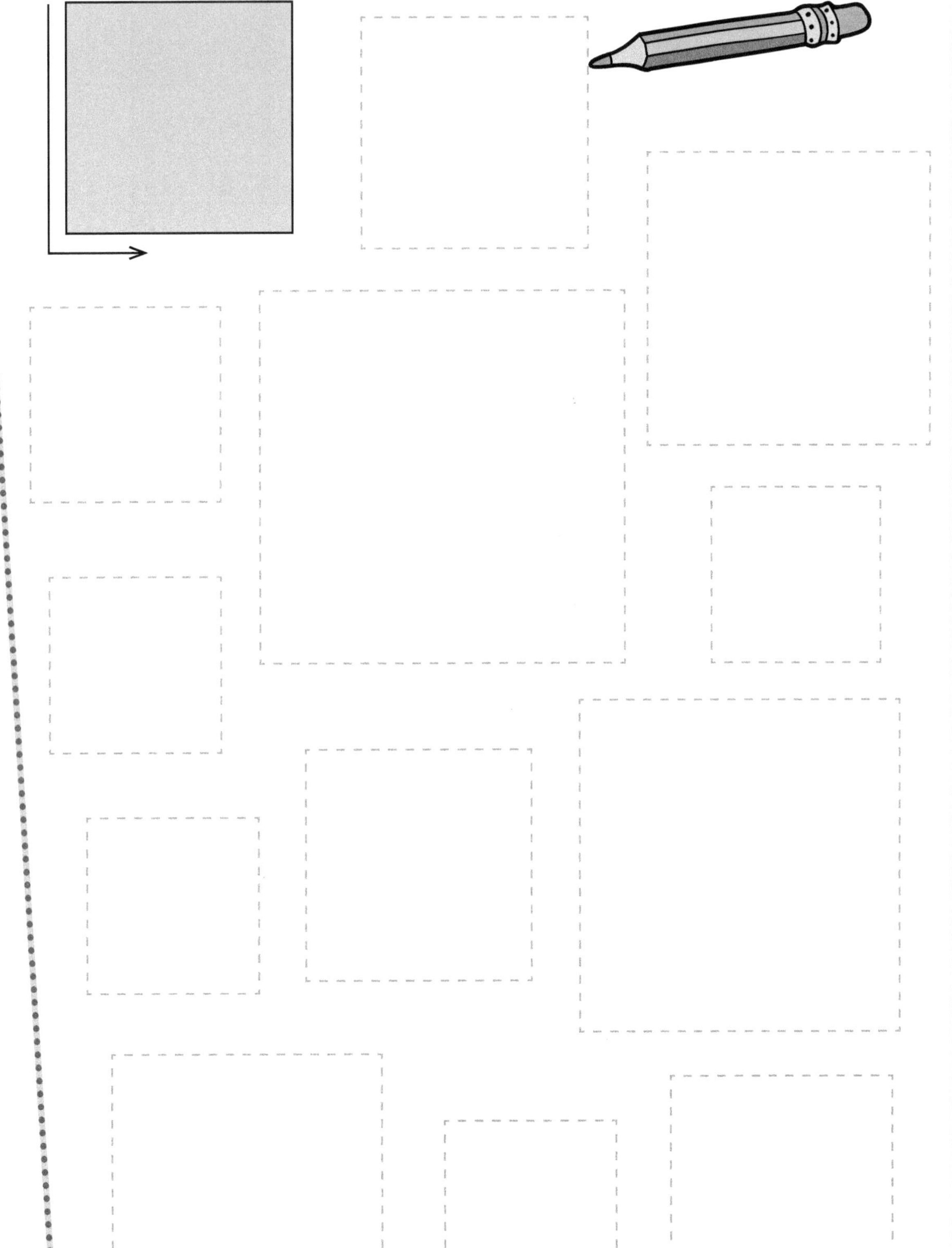

Directions: Trace the squares. Color the squares different colors.

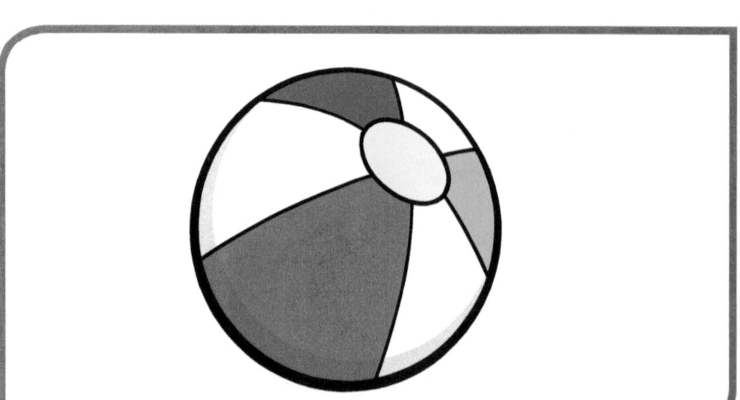

Directions: Count each group. Then, write the number of objects.

Directions: Circle all the little shoes. Color all the big shoes.

Directions: Draw a picture of what each community helper does.

Directions: Circle the baby that matches each parent.

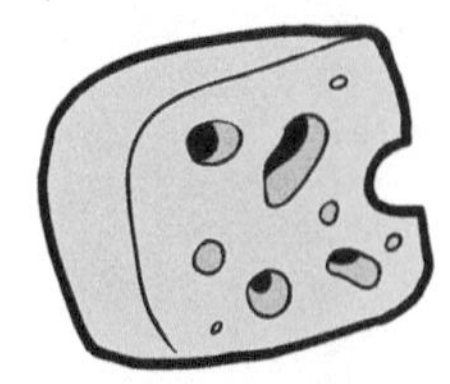

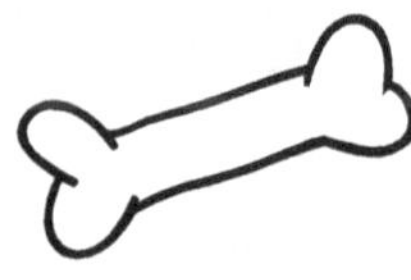

Directions: Name the animals. Name the foods. Draw a line from each animal to the food it eats.

Directions: Name all the objects on the page. Use blue to color anything that is blue in the real world.

Language Arts Activity

Have your child create a picture that has hidden letters in it. Have him or her put *A*s, *B*s, and *C*s in the picture. Then, have your child give the picture to a friend or family member and see whether that person can find the hidden letters.

Mathematics Activity

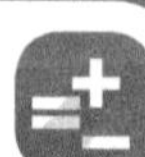

Help your child identify things to count at home, such as chairs, lamps, or books. Ask your child to select two items, draw them, and then count how many are in the house.

Science Activity

Have your child draw a picture of a farmyard with parent animals. Then, ask your child to add the baby animals. Tell your child that he or she can draw the babies near their parents, or he or she can draw a mixed-up farmyard where the babies are with the wrong parents!

Critical-Thinking Activity

Review page 34 with your child. Ask him or her to draw more matches that show other animals and what they eat.

Listening-and-Speaking Activity

Ask your child to make up a story about the blue ocean and the animals that live there. Ask your child to tell you his or her story.

Directions: Trace.

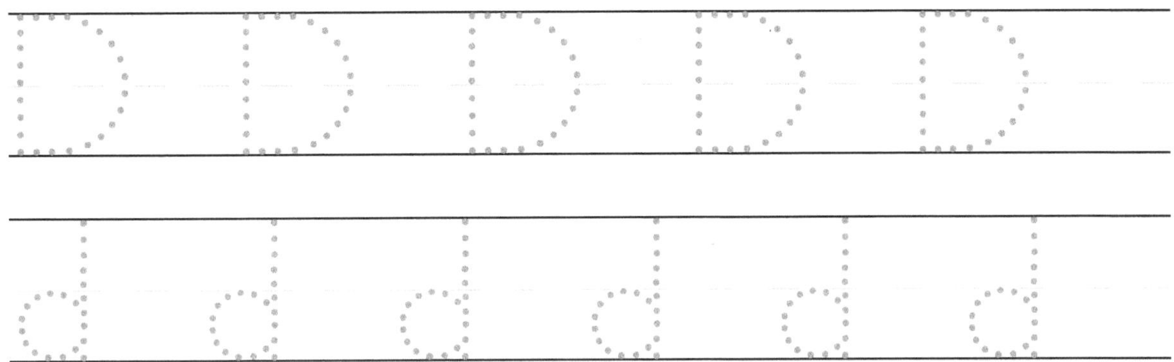

Directions: Write the letter Dd.

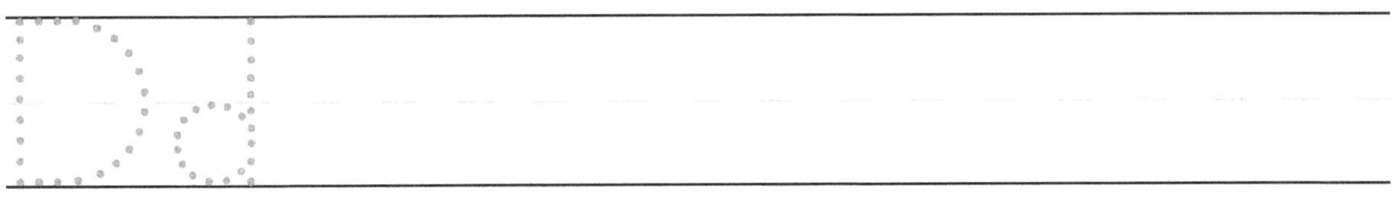

Directions: Say and trace.

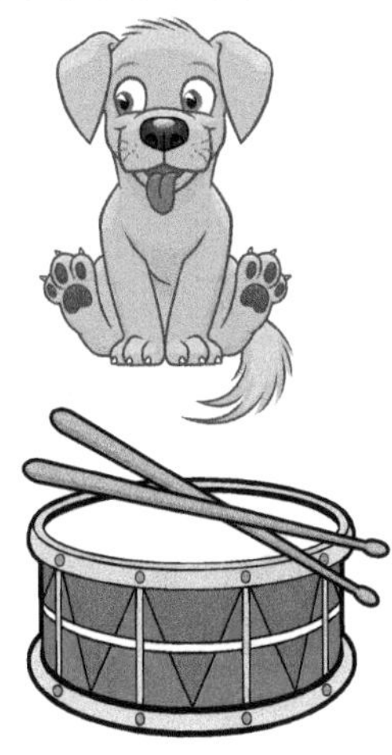

Directions: Trace.

Directions: Write the letter Ee.

Directions: Say and trace.

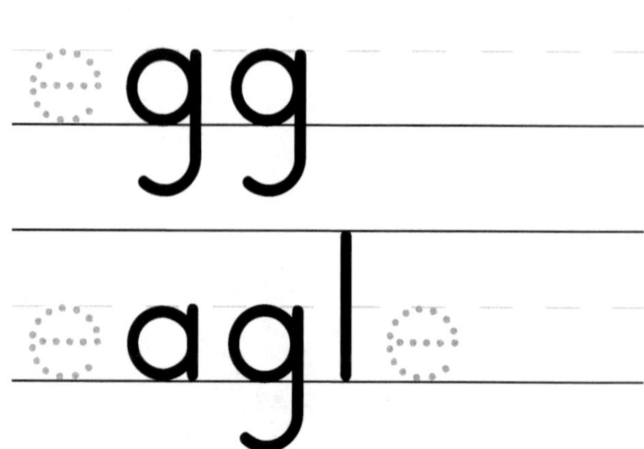

Directions: Trace.

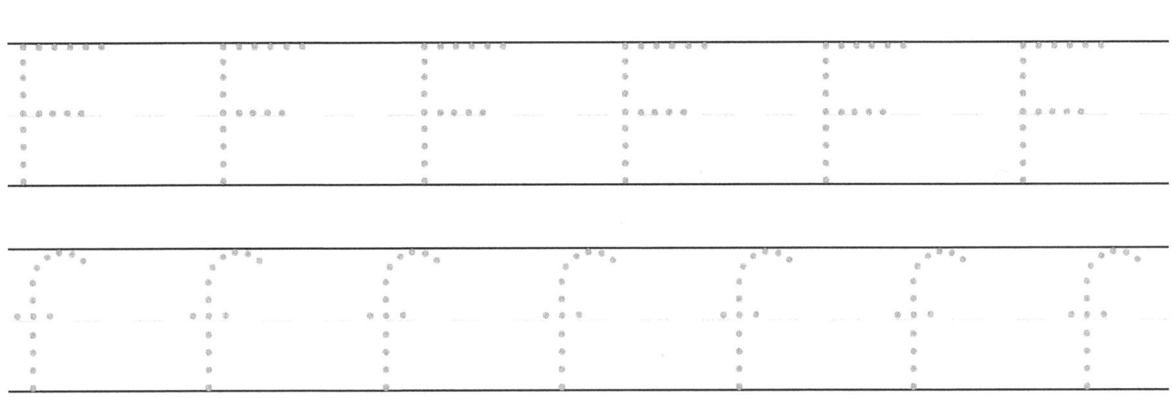

Directions: Write the letter Ff.

Directions: Say and trace.

Directions: Circle all the uppercase *D*s.

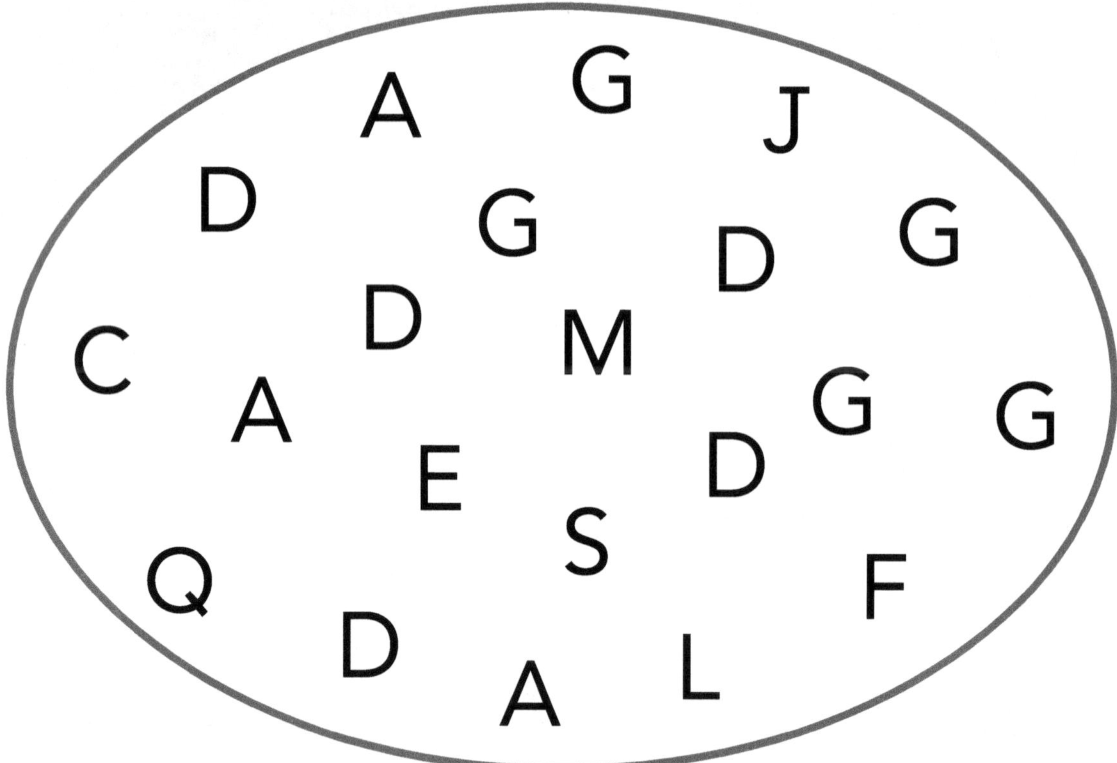

Directions: Circle all the uppercase *E*s.

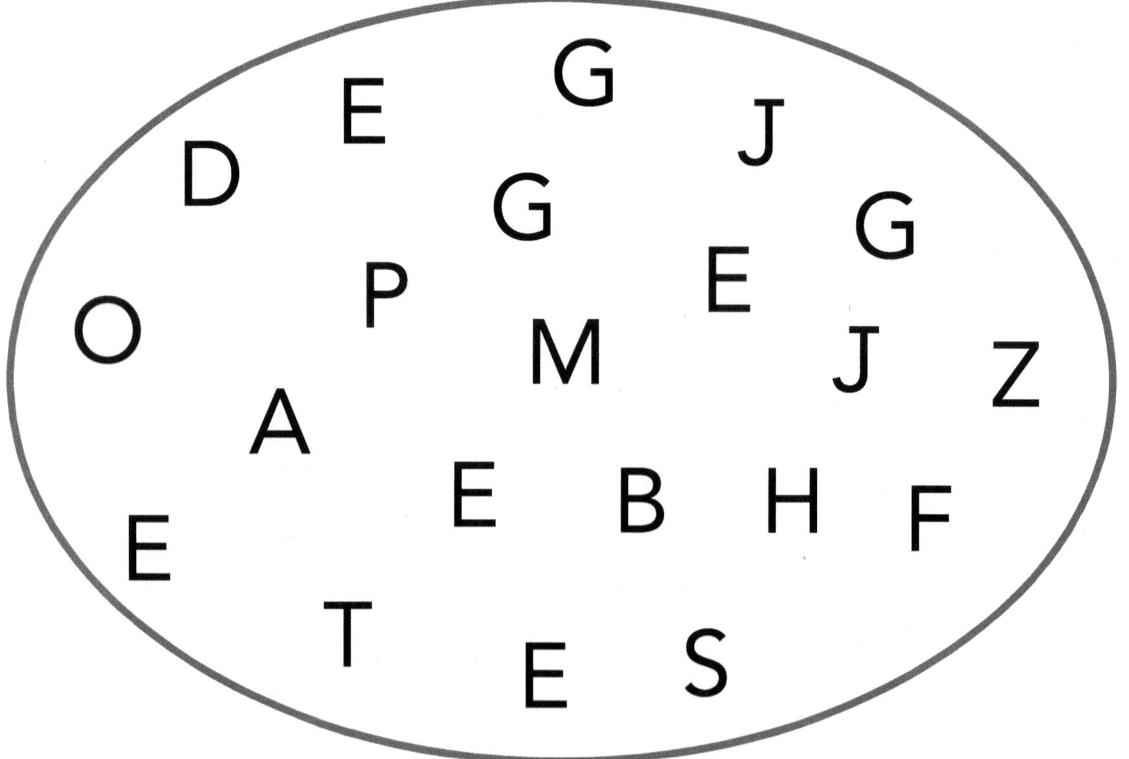

D

E

F

Directions: Say the letters on the left. Name the pictures on the right. Draw a line from each letter to the picture that begins with that letter's sound. Then, color the pictures.

friends

Directions: Draw a picture of your friends. Then, trace the word *friends*.

Directions: Trace.

3 3 3 3 3

Directions: Write the number 3.

3

Directions: Say and trace.

I see 3 dogs.

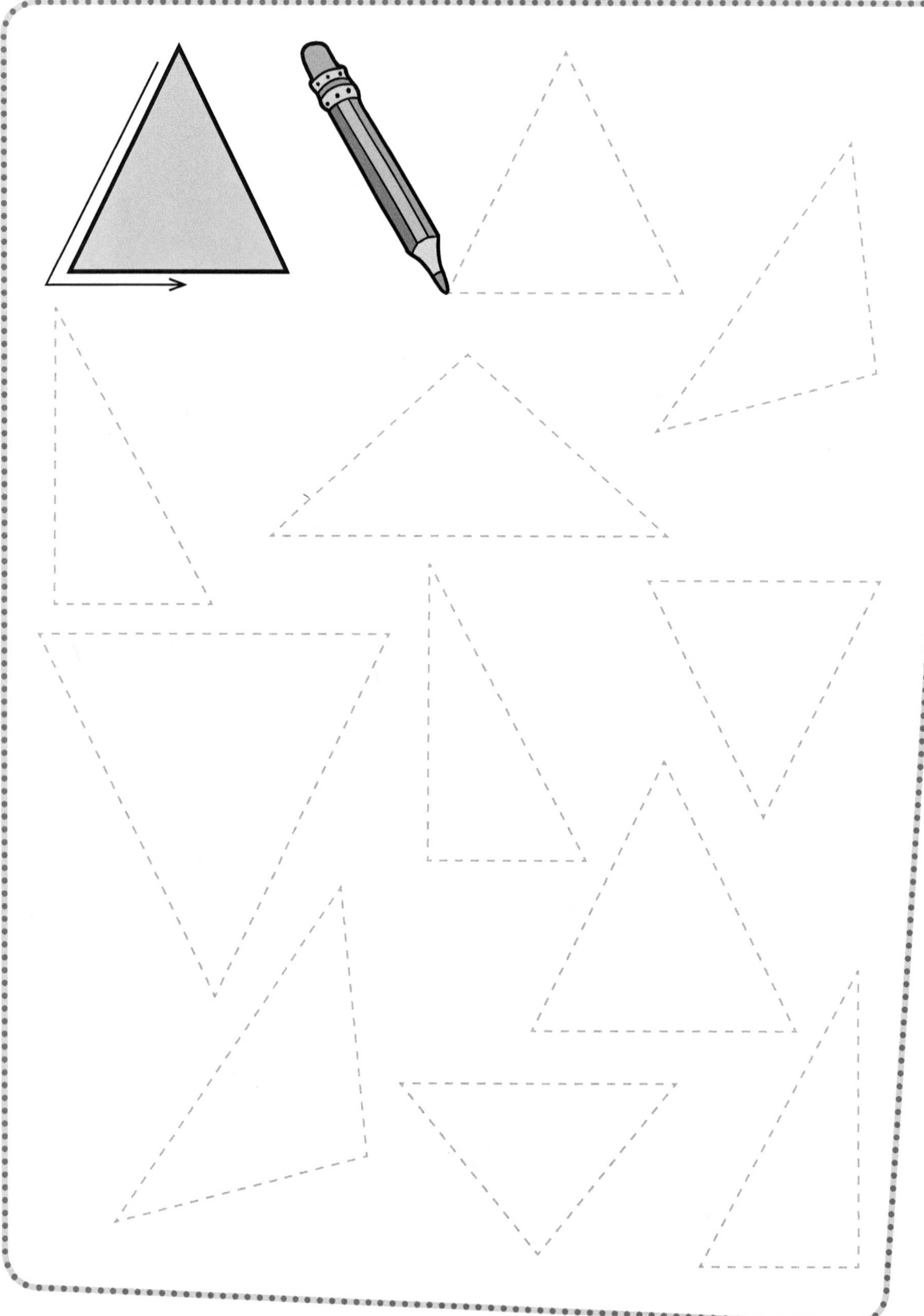

Directions: Trace the triangles. Color the triangles different colors.

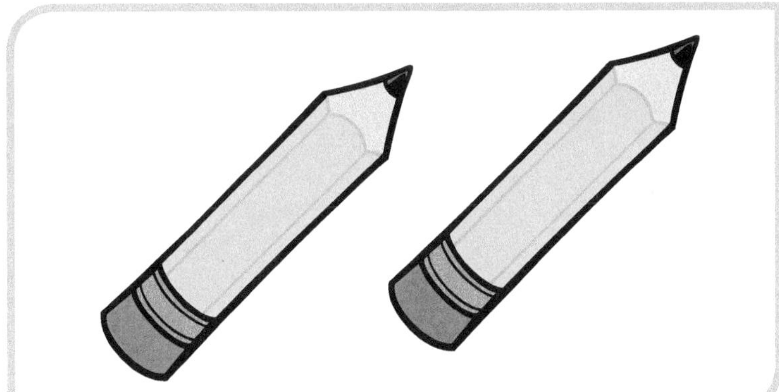

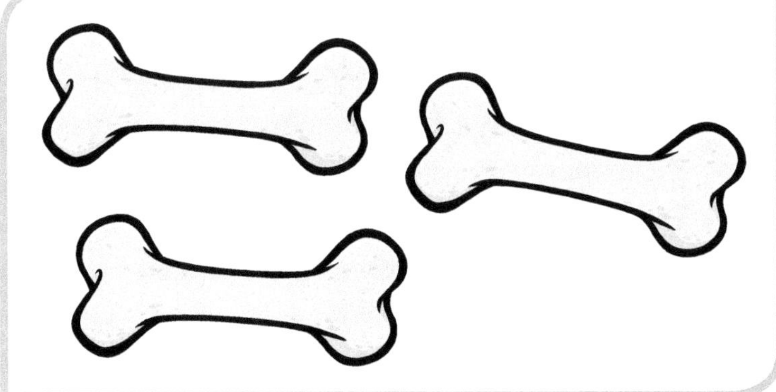

Directions: Count each group. Then, write the number of objects.

Directions: Color the largest objects red. Circle the medium objects. Color the smallest objects blue.

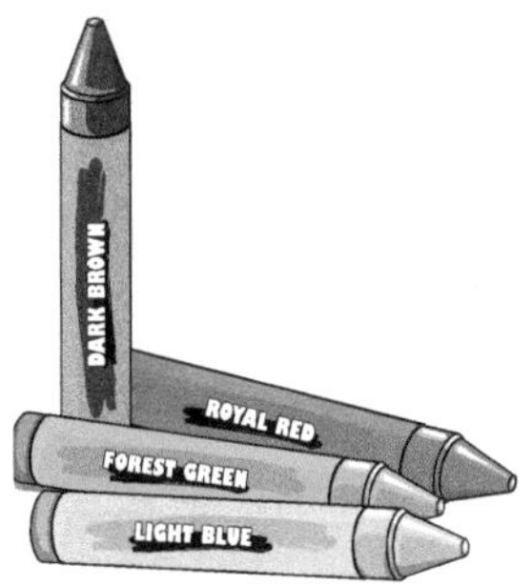

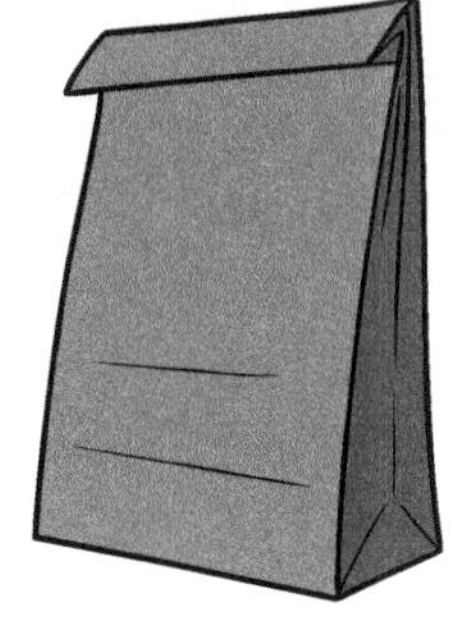

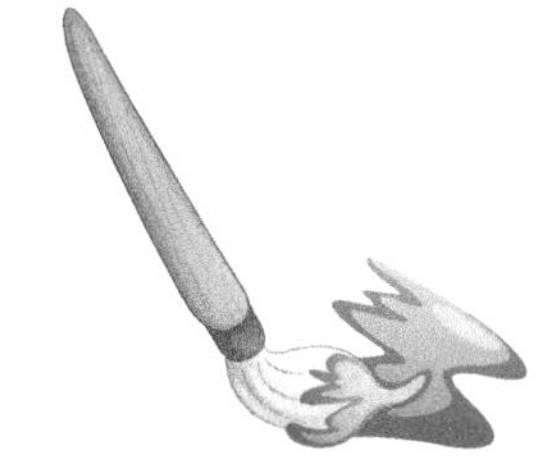

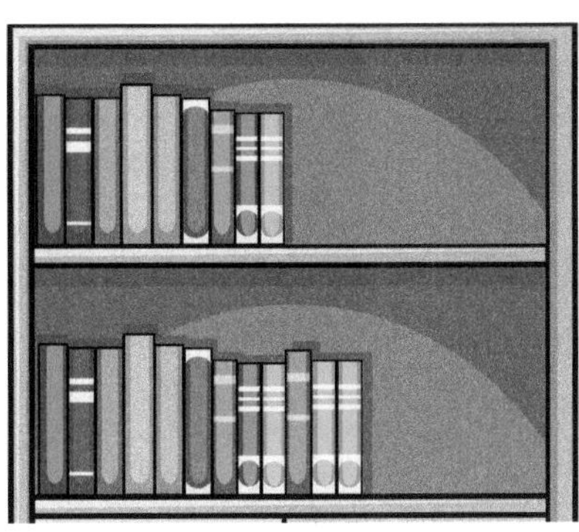

Directions: Draw a line from each school object to where it belongs.

Directions: Name each picture. Circle the items that are hot. Cross out the items that are cold.

Directions: Draw how Jack and Jill should get to the water.

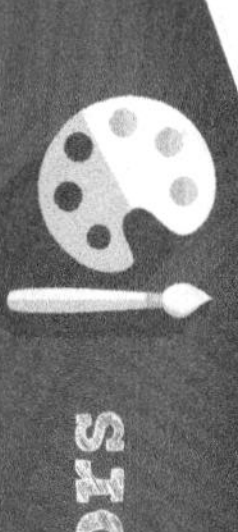

Directions: Name all the objects on the page. Use yellow to color anything that is yellow in the real world.

Language Arts Activity

Have your child write these words three times each: *bed, fed, bad, cab, face*. Have your child say the sound each letter makes as he or she writes it.

Mathematics Activity

Have your child draw a picture that has one circle, two squares, and three triangles. Have him or her color it using red, blue, and yellow crayons.

Science Activity

Have your child draw a picture of the sun. Around the sun, have your child draw as many "hot" things as he or she can think of. Then, have your child draw a picture of ice. Around the ice, have your child draw as many "cold" things as he or she can think of. Have your child write the names of any objects that he or she knows.

Critical-Thinking Activity

Have your child create his or her own maze for Jack and Jill. He or she can draw the maze on a separate sheet of paper. Encourage your child to ask a friend to try to solve it.

Listening-and-Speaking Activity

Ask your child to make up a story about living in a really hot or a really cold place. Ask your child to tell you his or her story. Ask your child questions about the story, such as *What would life be like there? How might people dress? How would it be different from living here?*

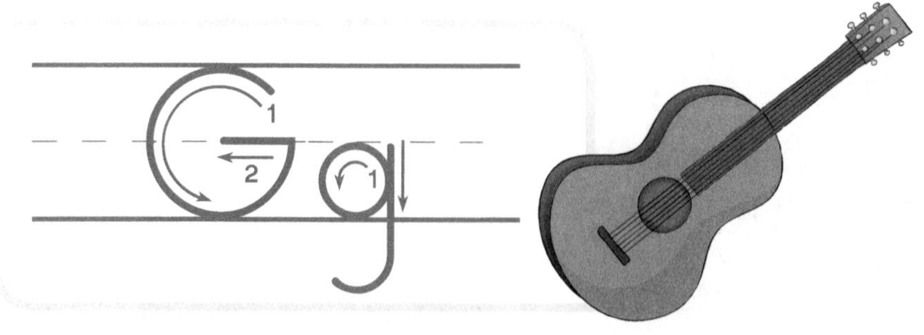

Directions: Trace.

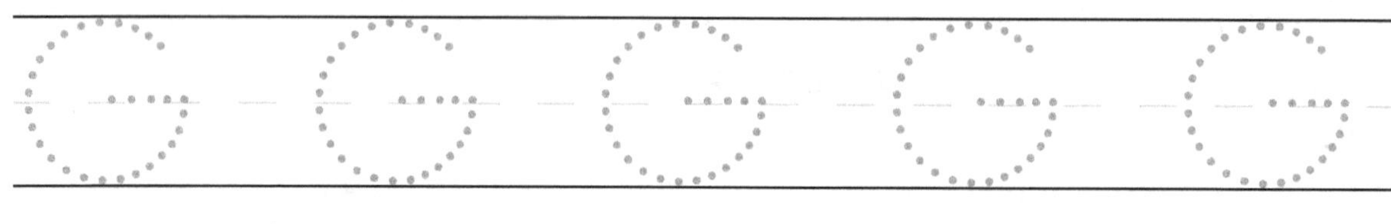

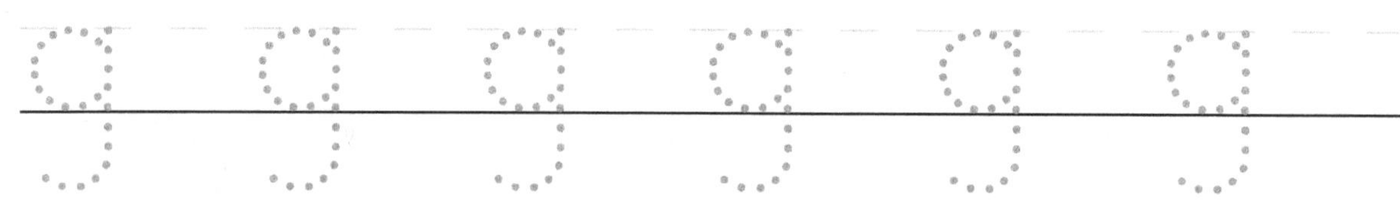

Directions: Write the letter Gg.

Directions: Say and trace.

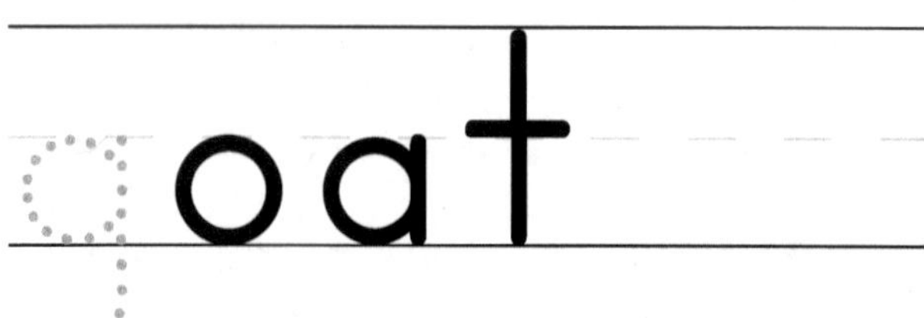

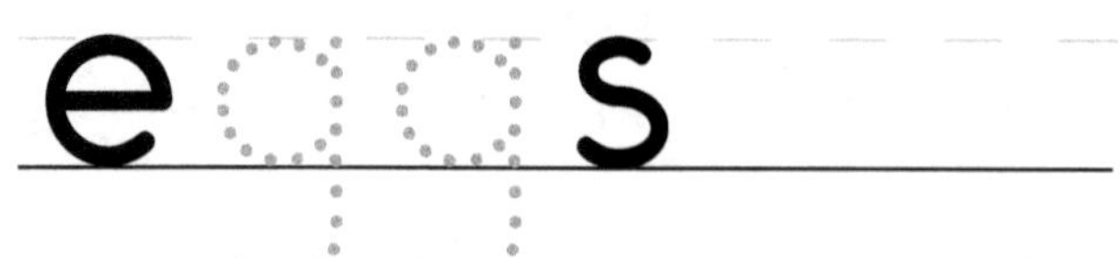

Directions: Trace.

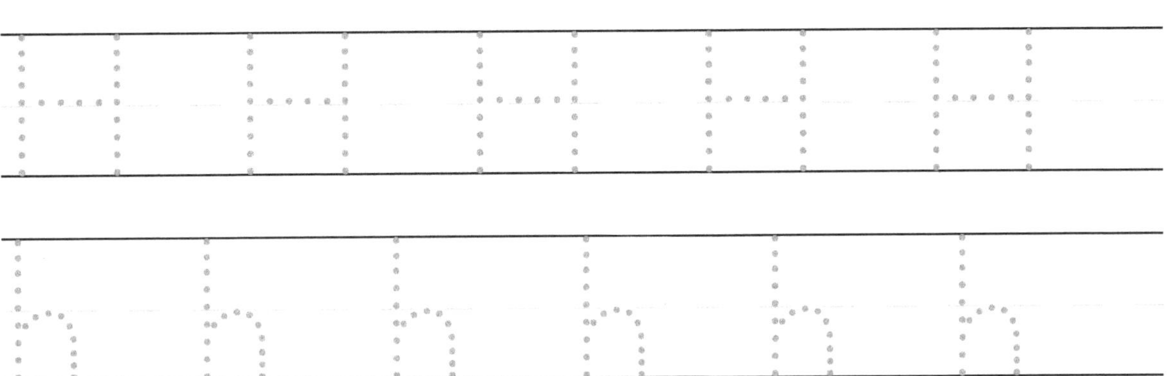

Directions: Write the letter Hh.

Hh

Directions: Say and trace.

horse

house

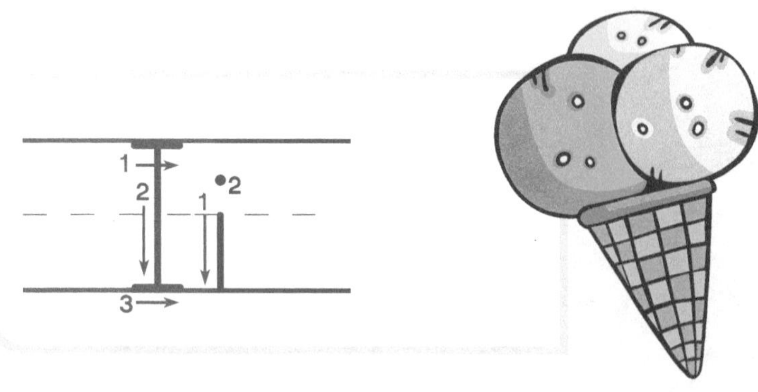

Directions: Trace.

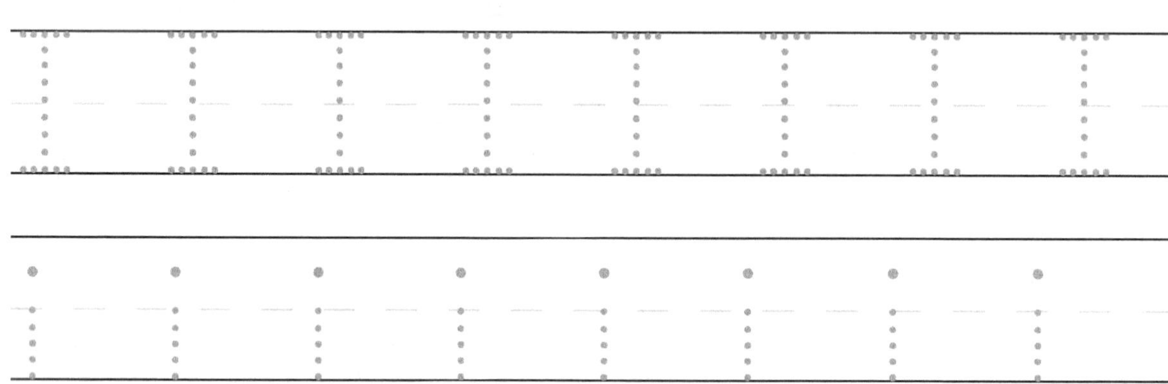

Directions: Write the letter Ii.

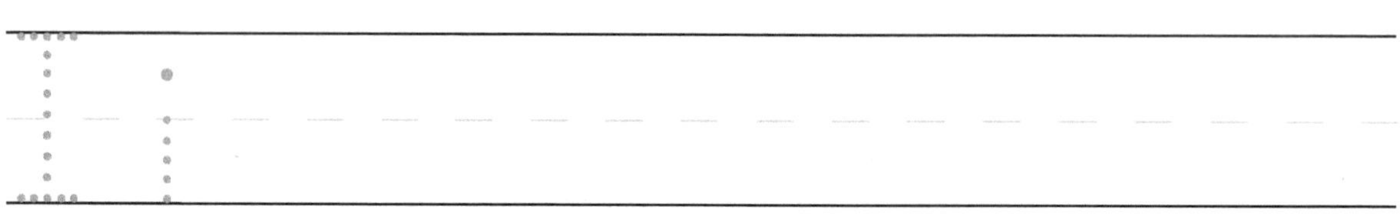

Directions: Say and trace.

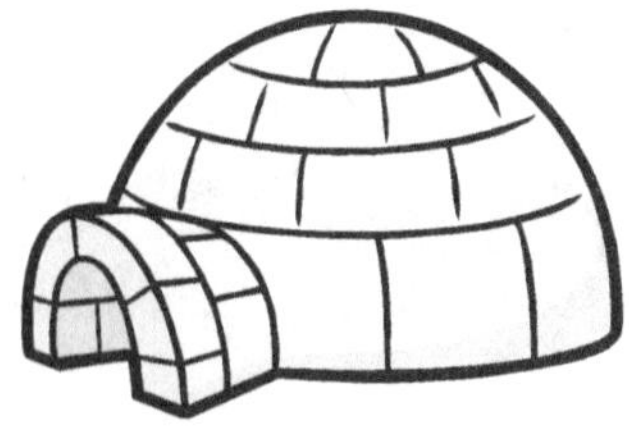

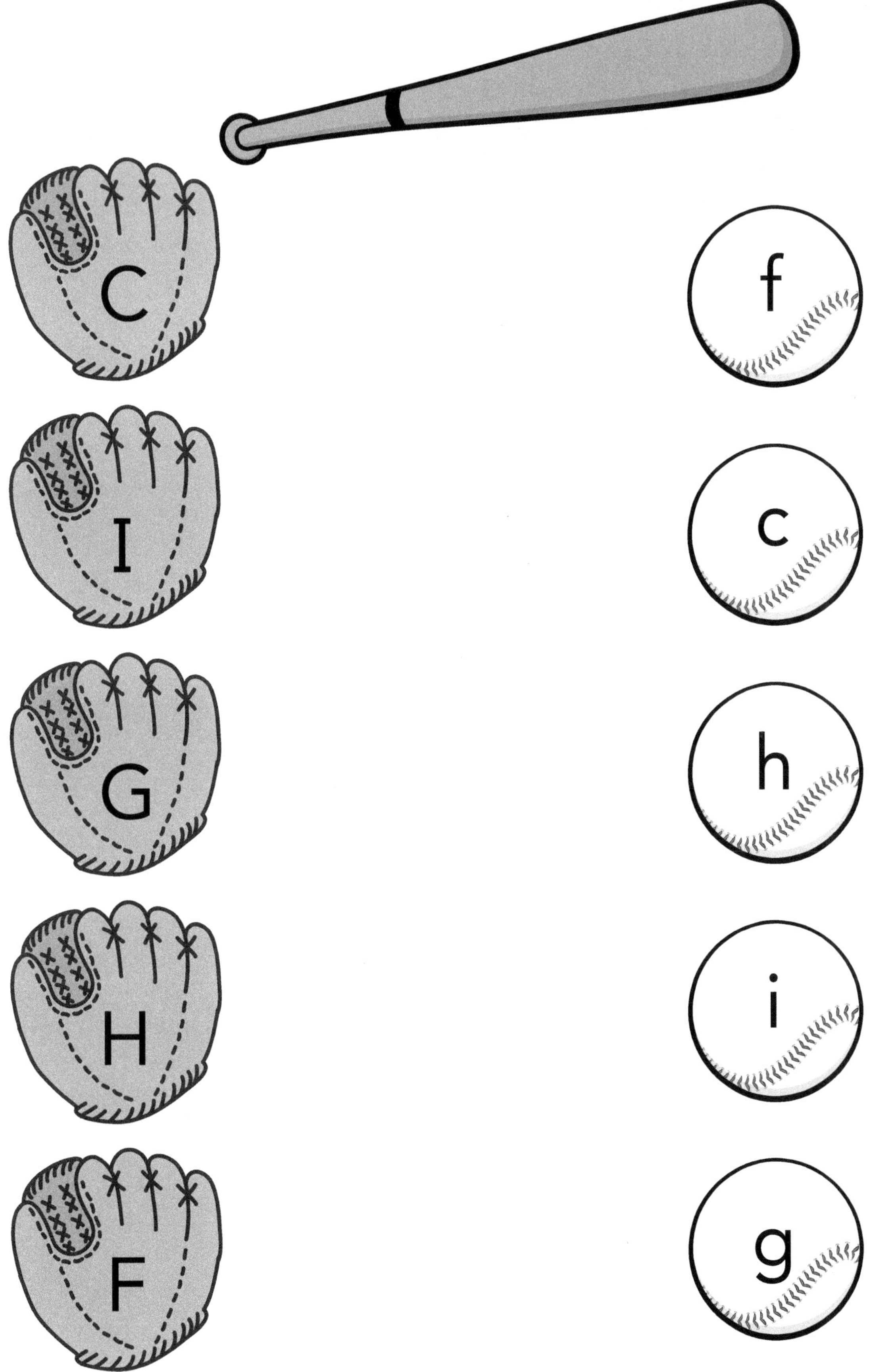

Directions: Match each glove to the ball with the same letter. Then, color the balls different colors!

Directions: Write the letter that you hear at the beginning of each word.

Directions: Draw a picture of your favorite animal. Then, write the name of the animal.

Directions: Trace.

4 4 4 4 4

Directions: Write the number 4.

4

Directions: Say and trace.

I see 4 horses.

Directions: Trace the rectangles. Color the rectangles different colors.

Directions: Draw 1 circle. ○

Directions: Draw 2 squares. □

Directions: Draw 3 triangles. △

Directions: Draw 4 rectangles. ▭

Directions: Draw the missing flowers.

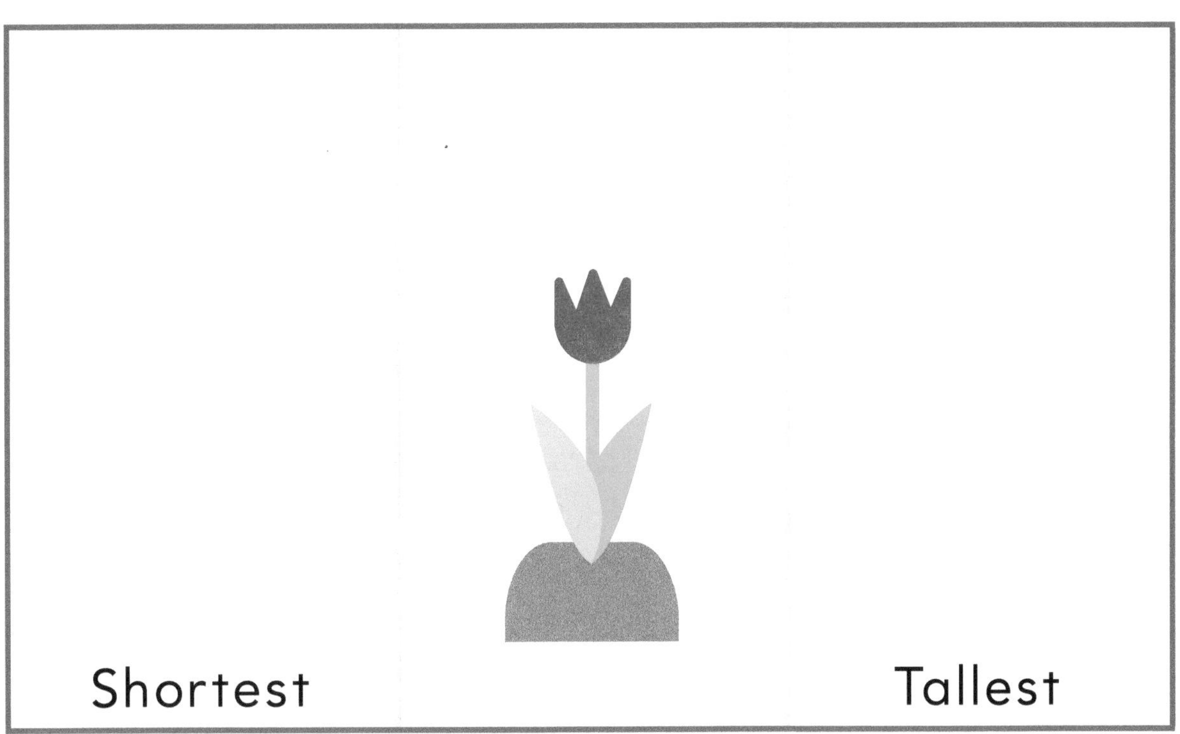

Directions: Draw the missing bears.

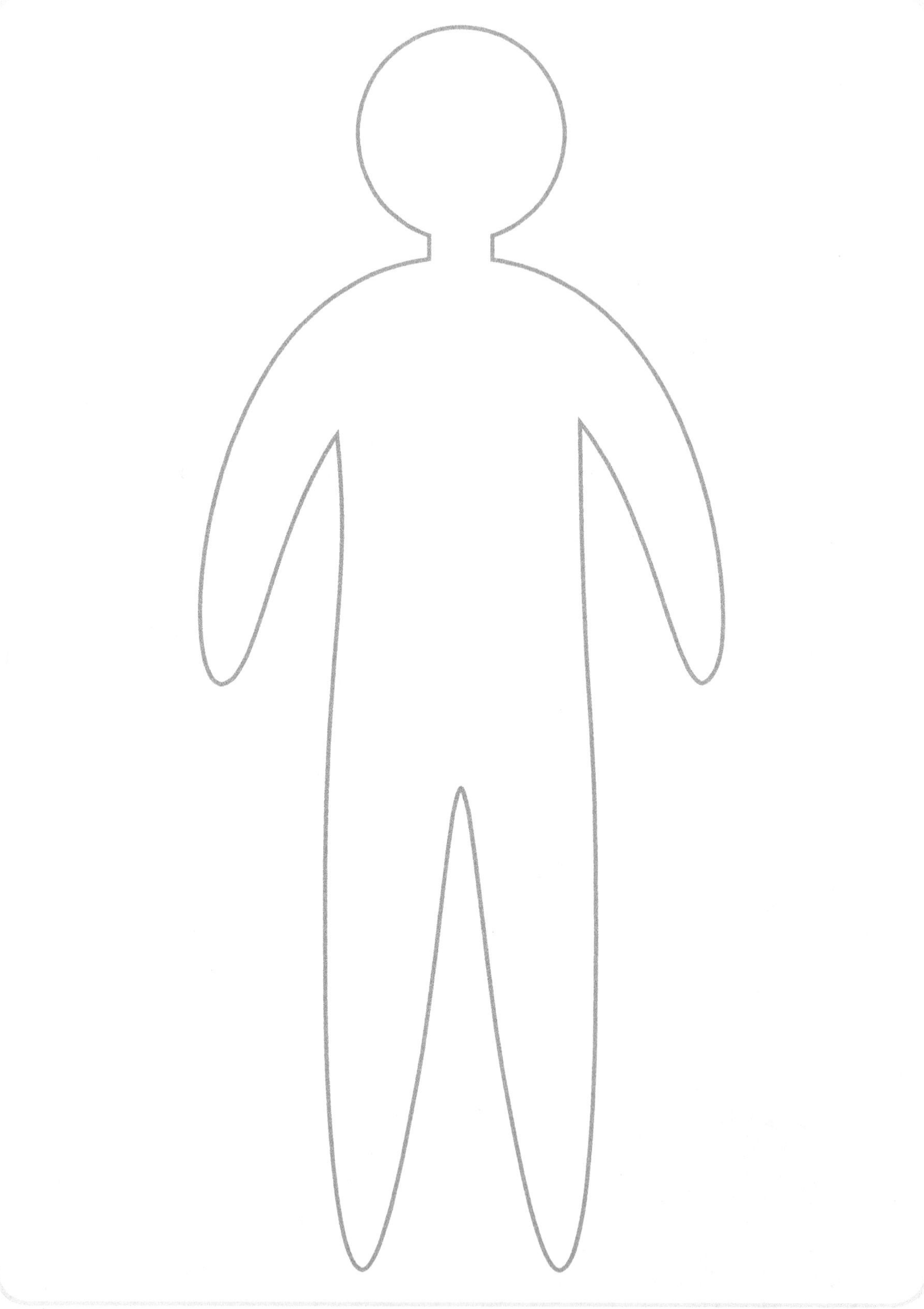

Directions: Draw an adult at work. Add lots of details to this outline. Make sure you think about the background. What is your adult doing?

Directions: Color the summer pictures yellow. Color the winter pictures blue.

Directions: Look at each row. Find the one that looks different. Tell how it is different and circle it.

Directions: Name all the objects on the page. Use green to color anything that is green in the real world.

Language Arts Activity

Have your child write the first nine letters of the alphabet three times each. Then, have your child write the letters three times each in silly writing, in different colors, or in fancy script.

Mathematics Activity

Help your child make a worksheet. Fold a sheet of paper in half. On one side, have your child draw groups of shapes, such as three circles or four triangles. Then, on the other side, have your child draw matching groups of animals, such as three birds or four ants. Finally, have your child draw lines to match the groups together.

Social Studies Activity

Ask your child to draw what he or she wants to be when he or she grows up. Have your child draw himself or herself as an adult doing that job. Encourage your child to include plenty of details in his or her drawing.

Critical-Thinking Activity

Ask your child to find a picture in this book. Have him or her draw a copy of that picture on another sheet of paper. Then, have him or her draw it again, but change one thing. Have your child give his or her drawing to a friend or family member to see whether that person can tell what your child changed.

Listening-and-Speaking Activity

Ask your child to make up a story about living in the green forest. Ask your child to tell you his or her story. Ask your child questions about the story, such as *What animals live with you? Are they your friends? What is the best part about living in the forest?*

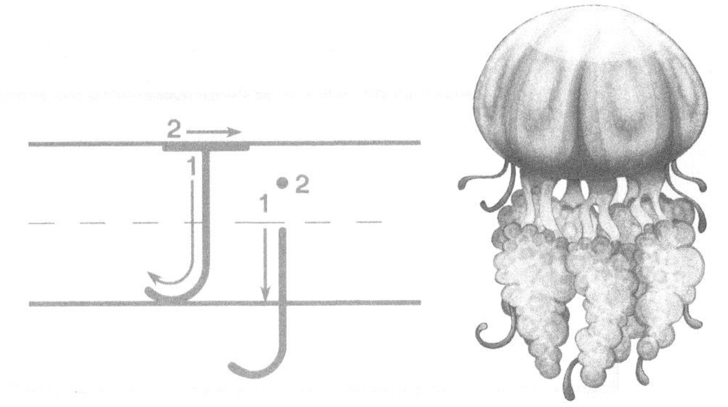

Directions: Trace.

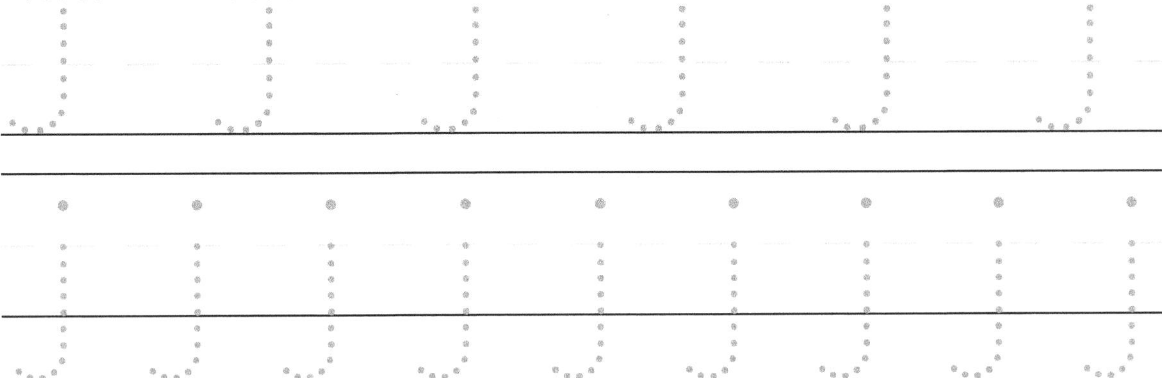

Directions: Write the letter Jj.

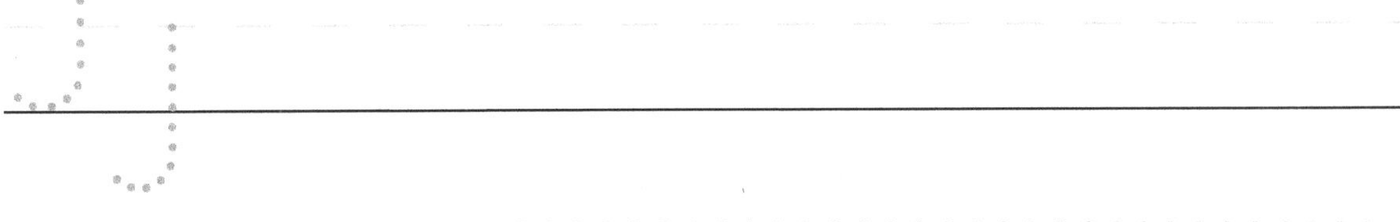

Directions: Say and trace.

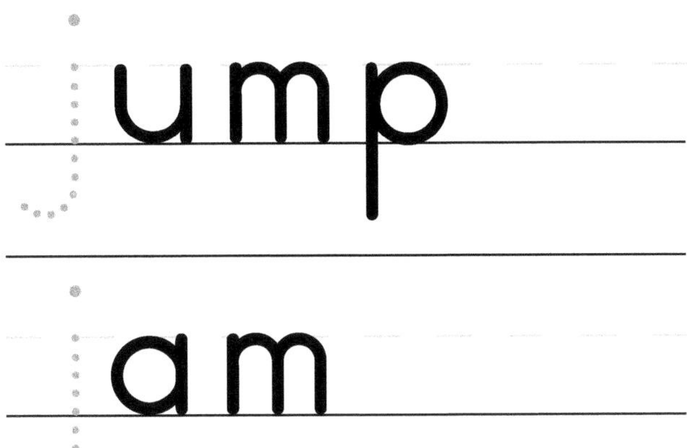

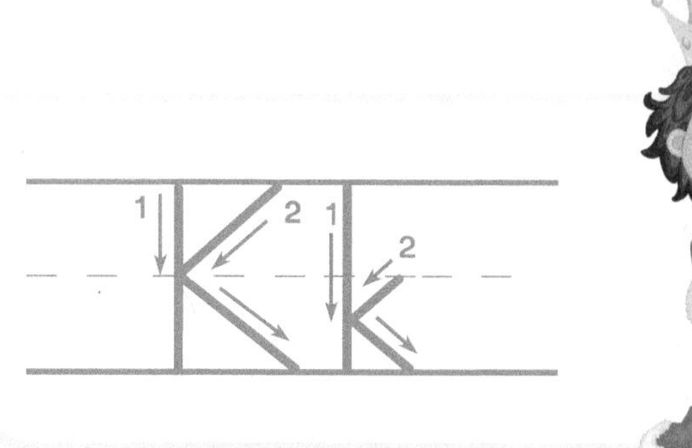

Directions: Trace.

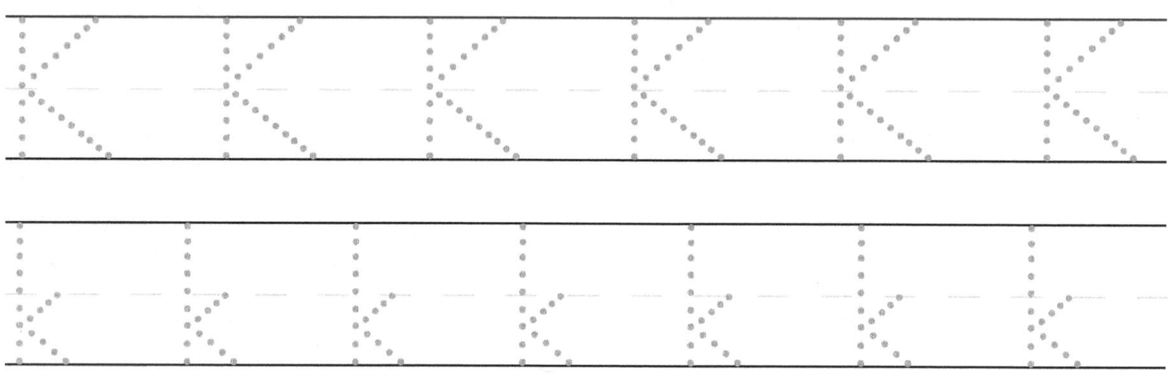

Directions: Write the letter Kk.

Directions: Say and trace.

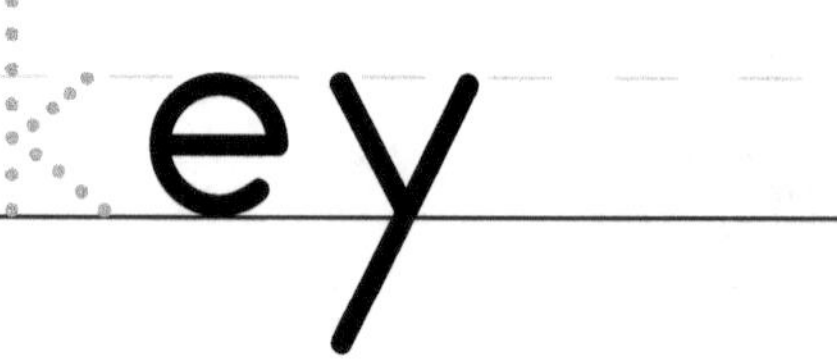

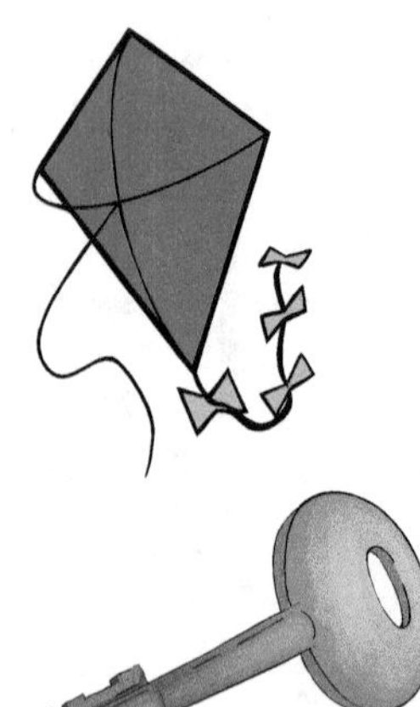

Directions: Trace.

Directions: Write the letter Ll.

Directions: Say and trace.

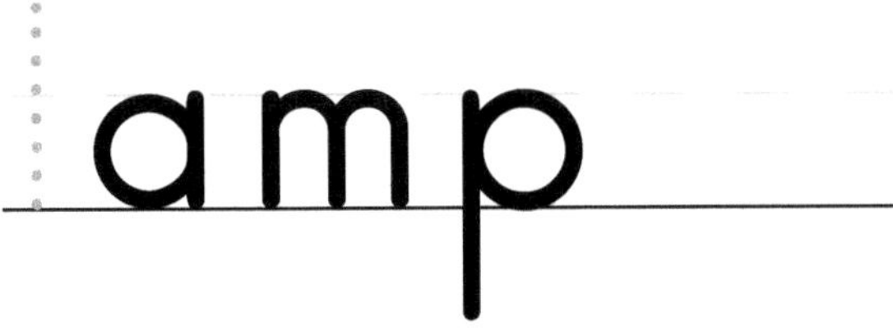

amp

ick

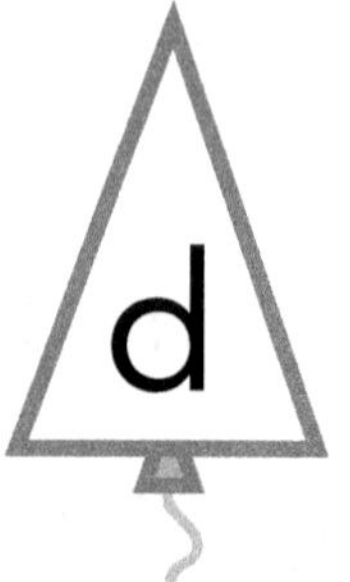

Directions: Draw a line from each uppercase letter to its lowercase partner. Then, color the pictures.

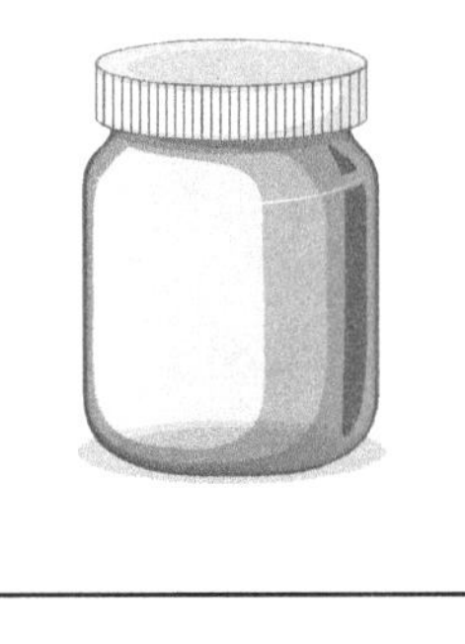

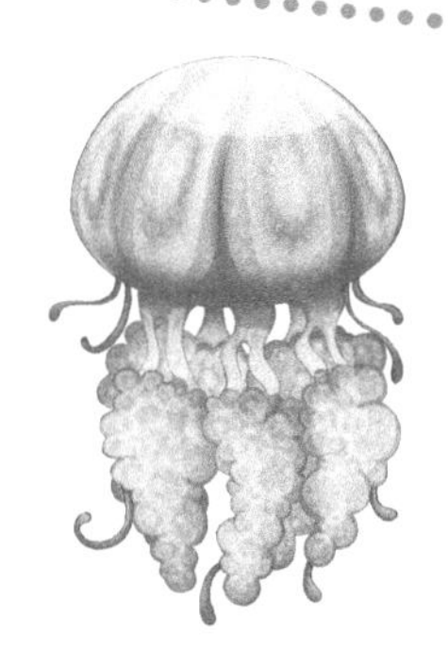

Directions: Write the letter that you hear at the beginning of each word.

Directions: Draw your favorite food. Then, write the name of the food.

Directions: Trace.

5 5 5 5 5

Directions: Write the number 5.

5

Directions: Say and trace.

I see 5 lamps.

Directions: Color the circles blue. Color the triangles green. Color the rectangles red.

Directions: Draw 3 circles. ○

Directions: Draw 4 squares. □

Directions: Draw 5 triangles. △

Directions: Draw 1 rectangle. ▭

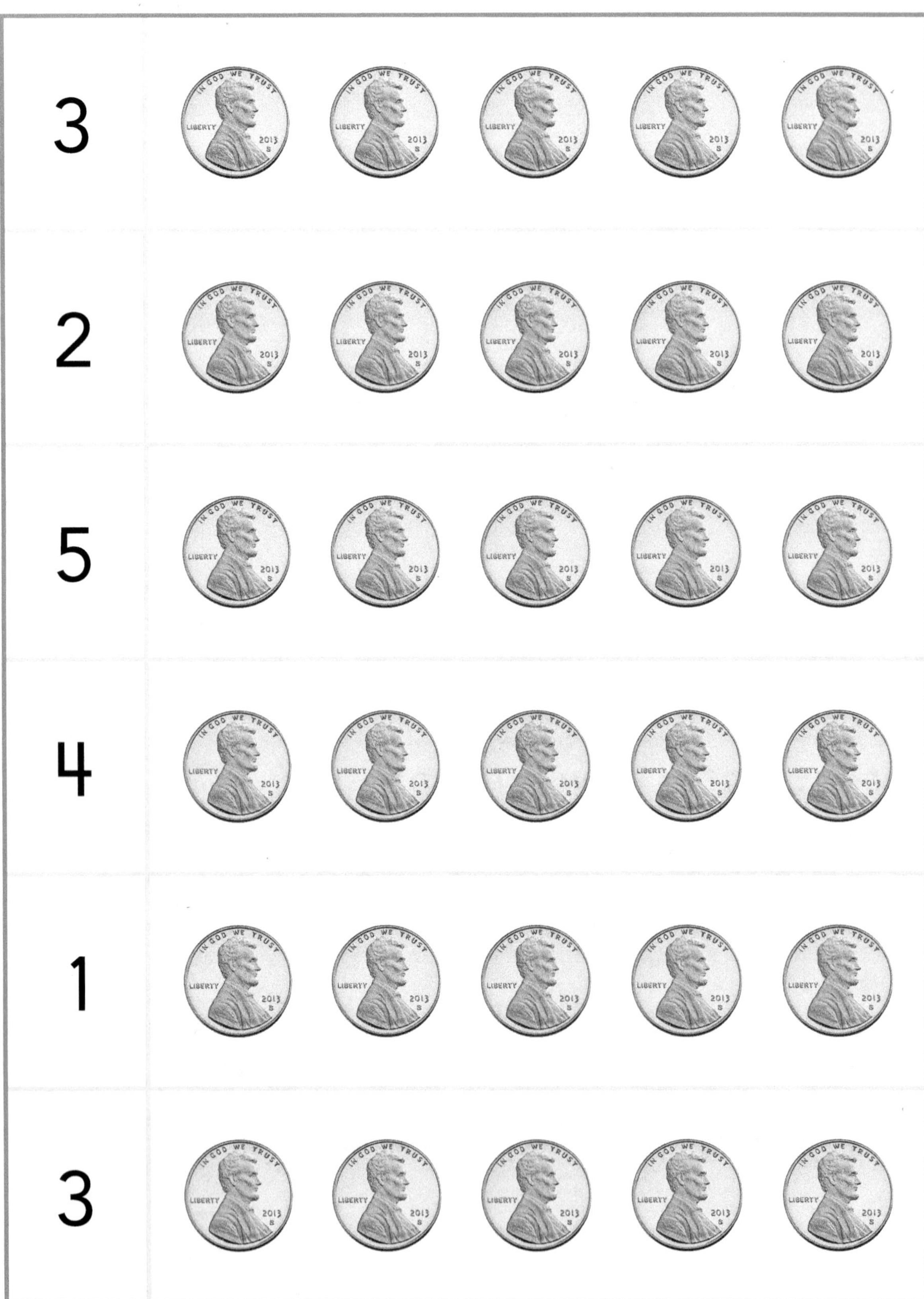

Directions: Look at the number at the beginning of each row. Circle that number of pennies.

Directions: Look for objects at home that begin with one of the letters in the magnifying glass. Draw what you find.

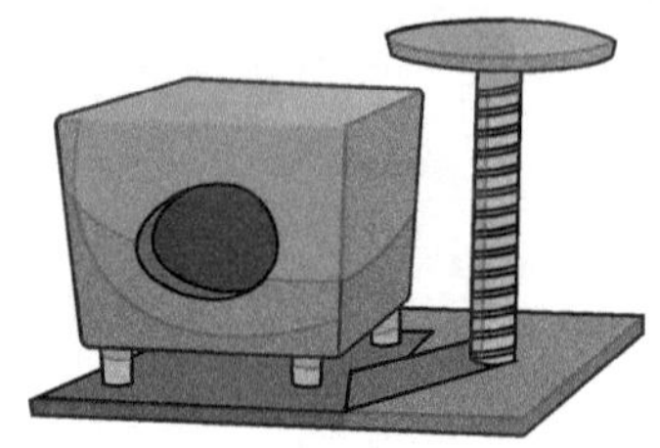

Directions: Draw a line from each animal to its home. Talk about your choices with a friend.

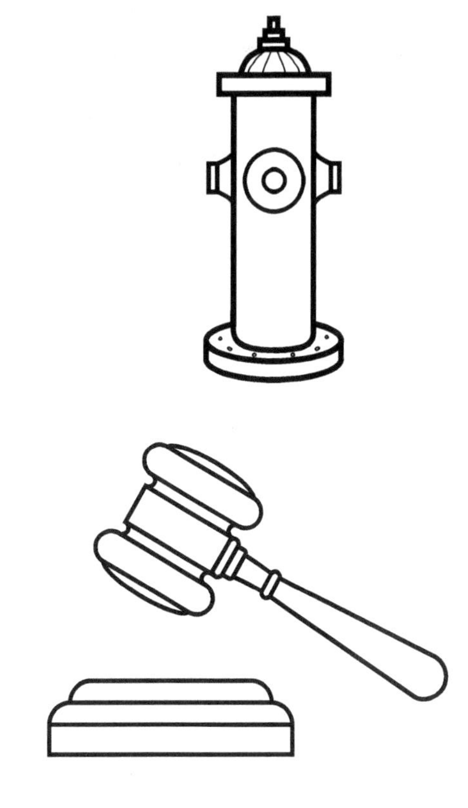

Directions: Match each person with the tool he or she uses. Then, color the tools.

Directions: Name all the objects on the page. Use orange to color anything that is orange in the real world.

Language Arts Activity

Have your child write these words three times each: *had, lad, kid, jab, hike.*

Mathematics Activity

Have your child look around the house to find things that come in fives, things that come in threes, or things that come in twos. Encourage your child to look in cabinets and dressers. Have your child write and draw to make a list of these items.

Science Activity

Have your child draw a picture of three different animals in their homes. Tell your child to draw one big animal, one medium animal, and one very small animal. Tell your child that each of the animal's homes will be different.

Critical-Thinking Activity

Ask your child what it would be like if everything in the world were orange. How would life be different? Have your child write and draw to make a list of five things that would be different.

Listening-and-Speaking Activity

Ask your child to make up a story about what it must be like to be an orange. Tell your child that an orange grows on a tree and then is picked one day. Ask your child what would happen to the orange. Encourage him or her to be creative. Then, ask your child to tell you his or her story.

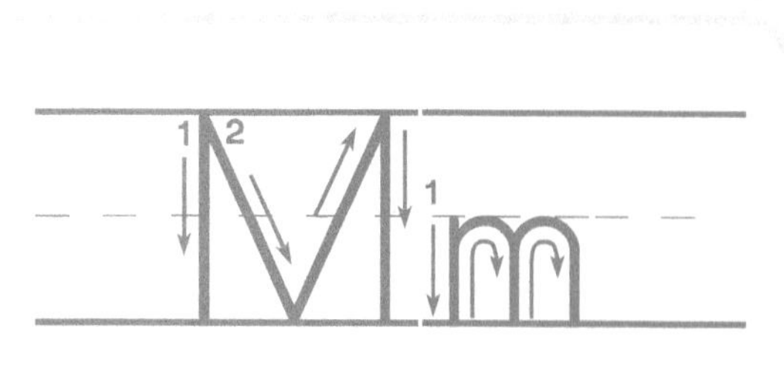

Directions: Trace.

M M M M M

m m m m m m

Directions: Write the letter Mm.

Mm

Directions: Say and trace.

map

man

Directions: Trace.

N N N N N N

n n n n n n

Directions: Write the letter Nn.

Nn

Directions: Say and trace.

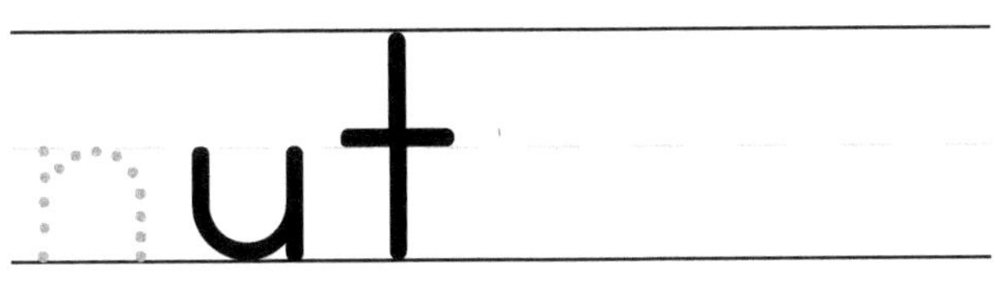

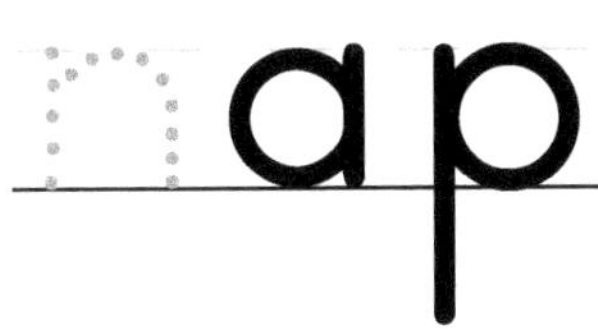

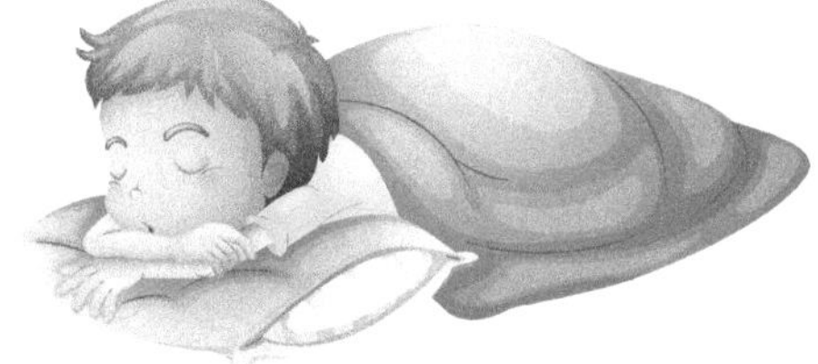

Directions: Trace.

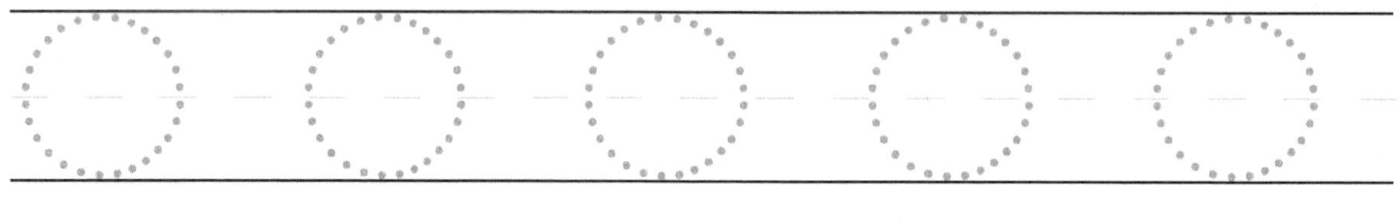

Directions: Write the letter Oo.

Directions: Say and trace.

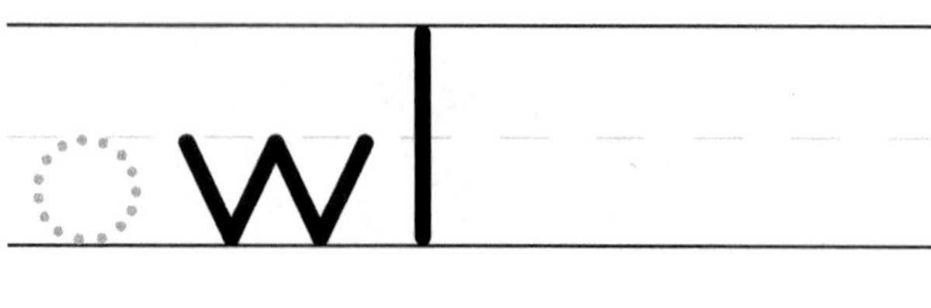

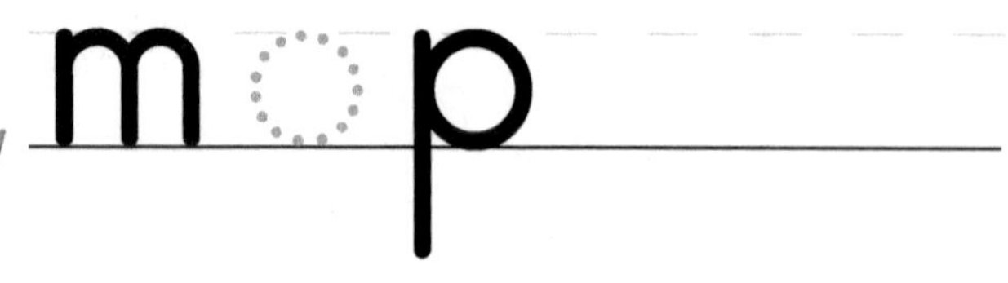

M	M	O	M	O	N		
o	n	o	n	m	n	o	m
n	n	o	n	m	n	o	m
m	o	m	n	n	o	m	o
O	N	M	O	N	O		
N	M	O	N	O	N		

Directions: Circle the letters that match the letter in the left column.

Directions: Color the picture in each row that starts with the letter on the left.

Directions: Draw your favorite toy. Then, write the name of the toy.

Directions: Trace.

6 6 6 6 6

Directions: Write the number 6.

6

Directions: Say and trace.

I see 6 owls.

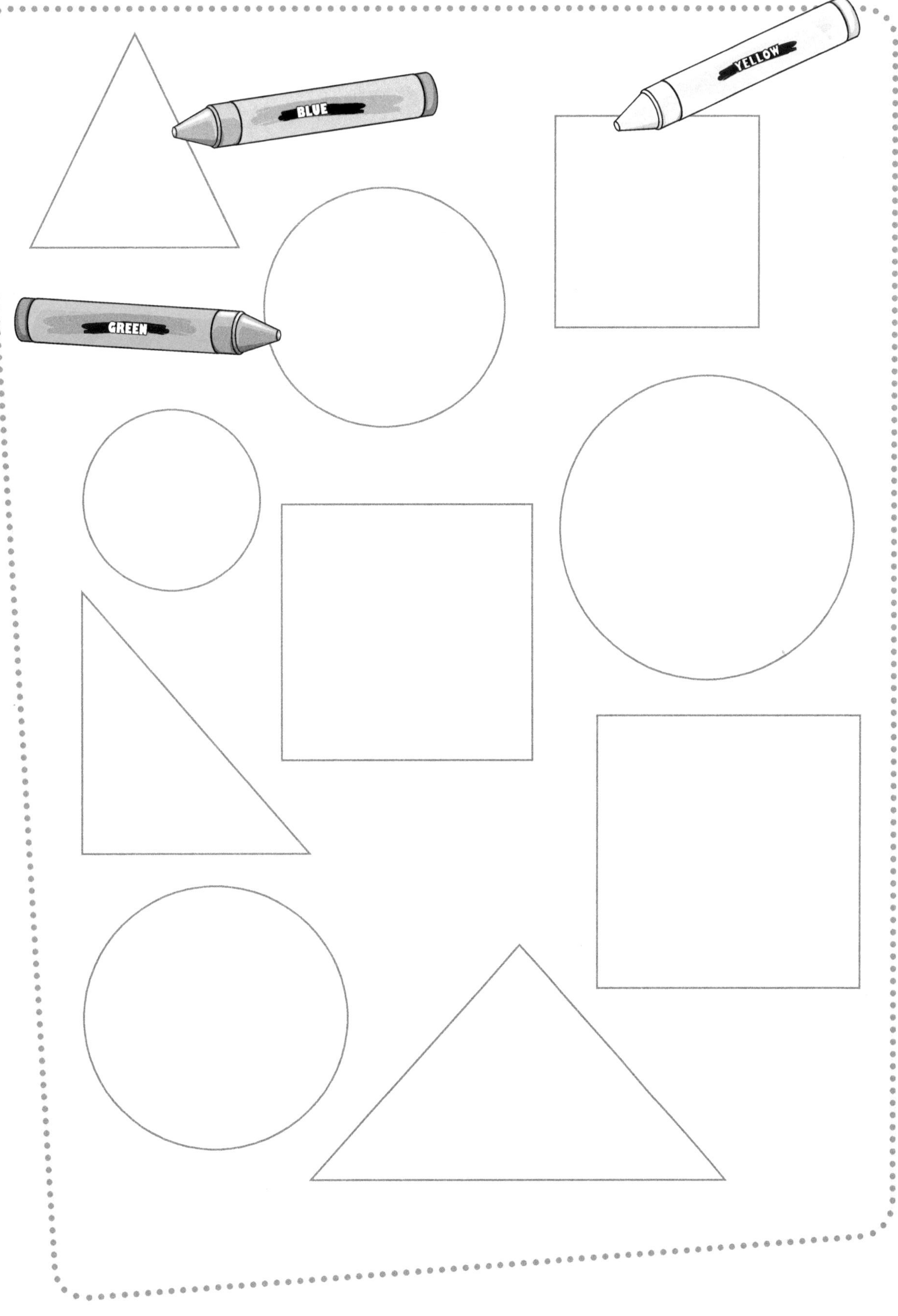

Directions: Color the squares yellow. Color the circles green. Color the triangles blue.

Directions: Draw a picture with 6 ◯, 5 □, 4 △, and 3 ▭.

Directions: Draw lines to connect matching groups of nickels.

Directions: Draw pictures of three rules you have to follow at home.

Directions: Pick two seasons. Draw a picture of a tree for each season.

Directions: Circle the lighter object on each scale.

Directions: Name all the objects. Use purple to color anything that is purple in the real world.

Directions: Start at the top and color this rainbow. Use red, orange, yellow, green, blue, and purple.

Language Arts Activity

Have your child practice writing the first 15 letters of the alphabet. Tell him or her to write the lowercase and uppercase of each letter using different colors.

Mathematics Activity

Have your child write the numbers 1 to 6. Then, have your child practice making new numbers, such as 11, 12, 13, 14, 15, and 16.

Social Studies Activity

Ask your child to think about somewhere other than home that has rules. Have your child draw three pictures to show those rules. Then, review the pictures your child drew on page 92. Ask your child how the rules at home are similar to and different from the rules at the place he or she chose.

Critical-Thinking Activity

Ask your child to select two objects from around the house. Have him or her hold one object in each hand and determine which one is heavier. Have your child do this a few times with different objects.

Listening-and-Speaking Activity

Ask your child to make up a story about what he or she finds at the end of a rainbow. Have your child tell you his or her story. Ask questions such as *Are you alone, or do you have friends with you? How do you feel when you get to the end of the rainbow?*

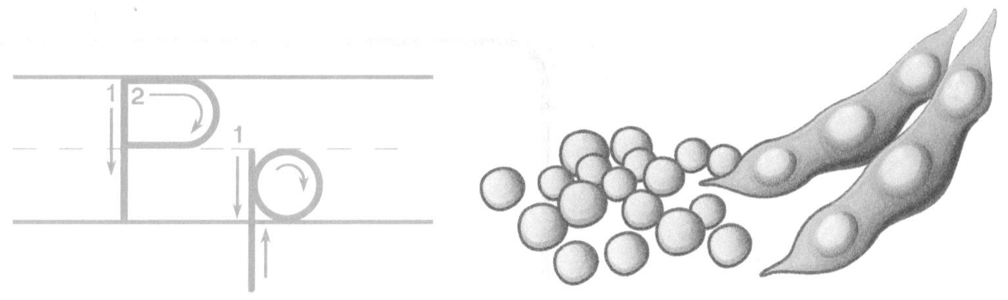

Directions: Trace.

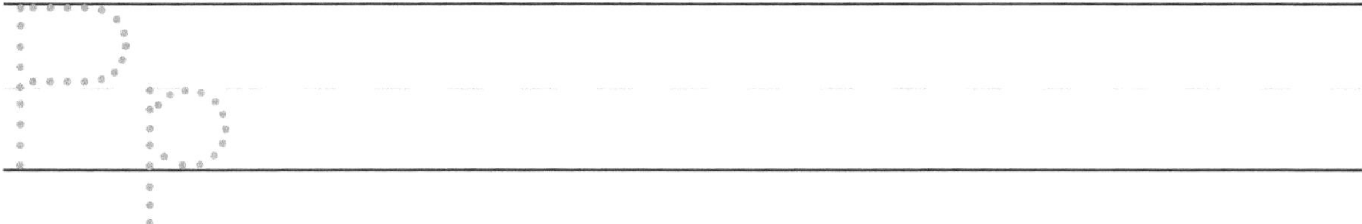

Directions: Write the letter Pp.

Directions: Say and trace.

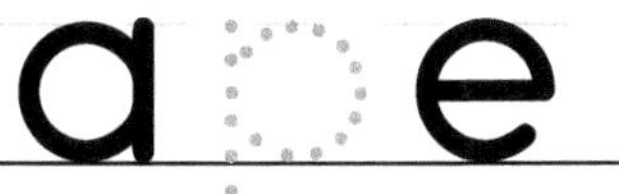

Directions: Trace.

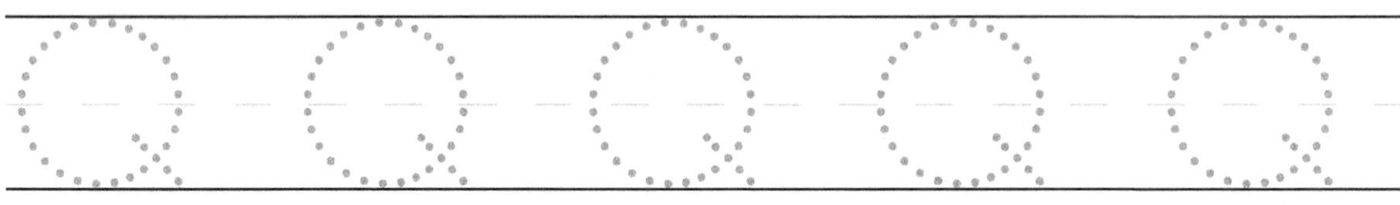

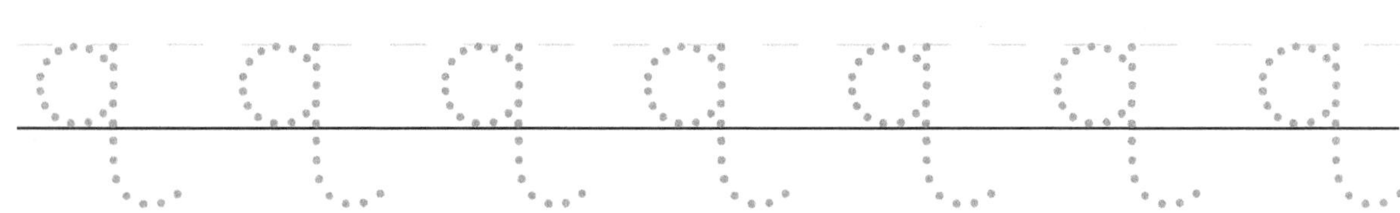

Directions: Write the letter Qq.

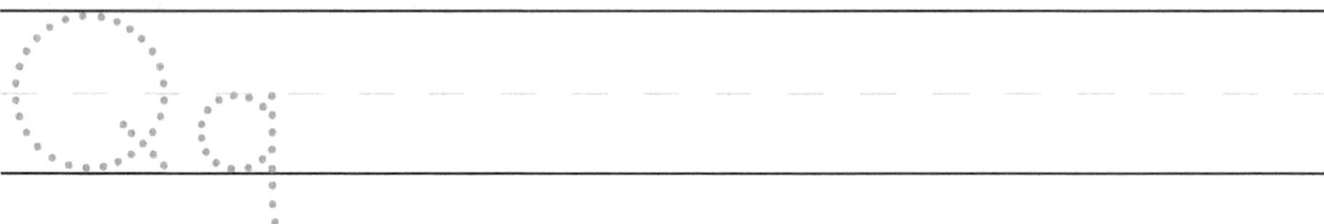

Directions: Say and trace.

queen

equal

Directions: Trace.

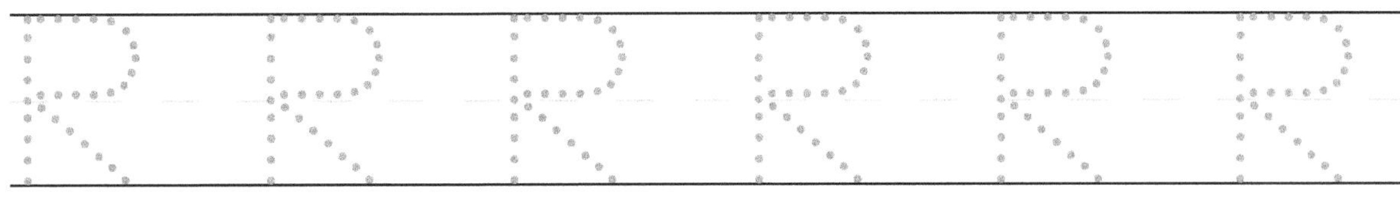

Directions: Write the letter Rr.

Directions: Say and trace.

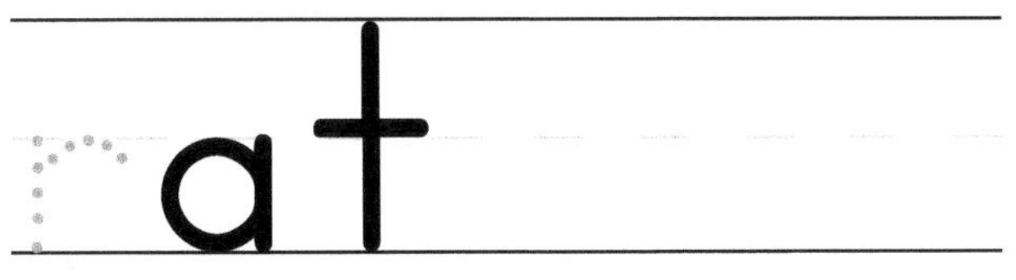

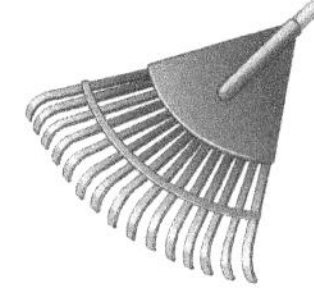

P	P	Q	R	P	R		
Q	R	Q	P	Q	P		
r	r	q	r	p	r	q	p
q	q	p	r	r	q	p	q
p	r	p	q	p	r	q	p
R	P	Q	R	Q	R		

Directions: Circle the letters that match the letter in the left column.

Directions: Color the picture in each row that starts with the letter on the left.

Directions: Draw your favorite place to play. Write the name of that place.

Directions: Trace.

Directions: Write the number 7.

Directions: Say and trace.

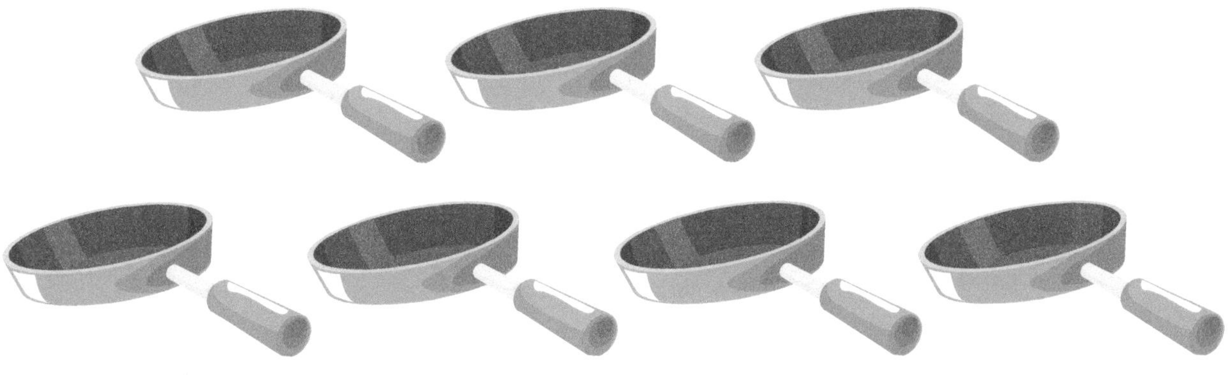

I see 7 pans.

Directions: Trace each row of shapes. Then, color the shapes in a pattern.

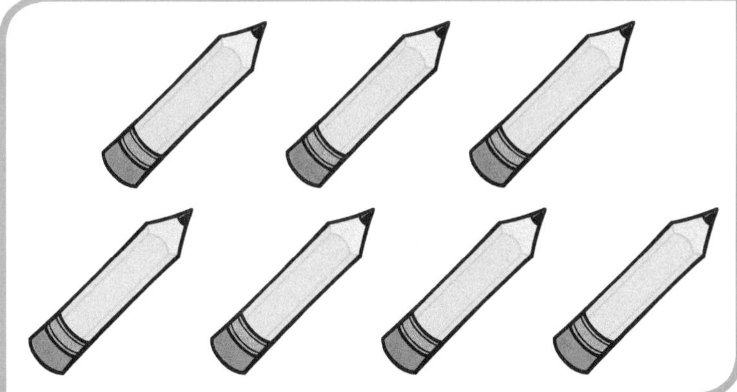

Directions: Count each group. Then, write the number of objects.

Mathematics

$2 + 1 =$ ______

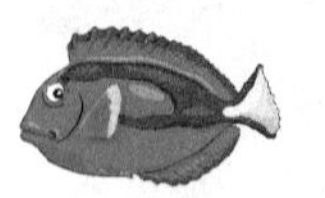

$5 + 1 =$ ______

$3 + 2 =$ ______

$2 + 2 =$ ______

Directions: Add the objects.

I like to help

.

Directions: Draw a picture of you helping someone. Trace the words. Then, write that person's name.

Directions: Look at each row of pictures. Each row has the number 1. Write the numbers 2 and 3 to put the pictures in order.

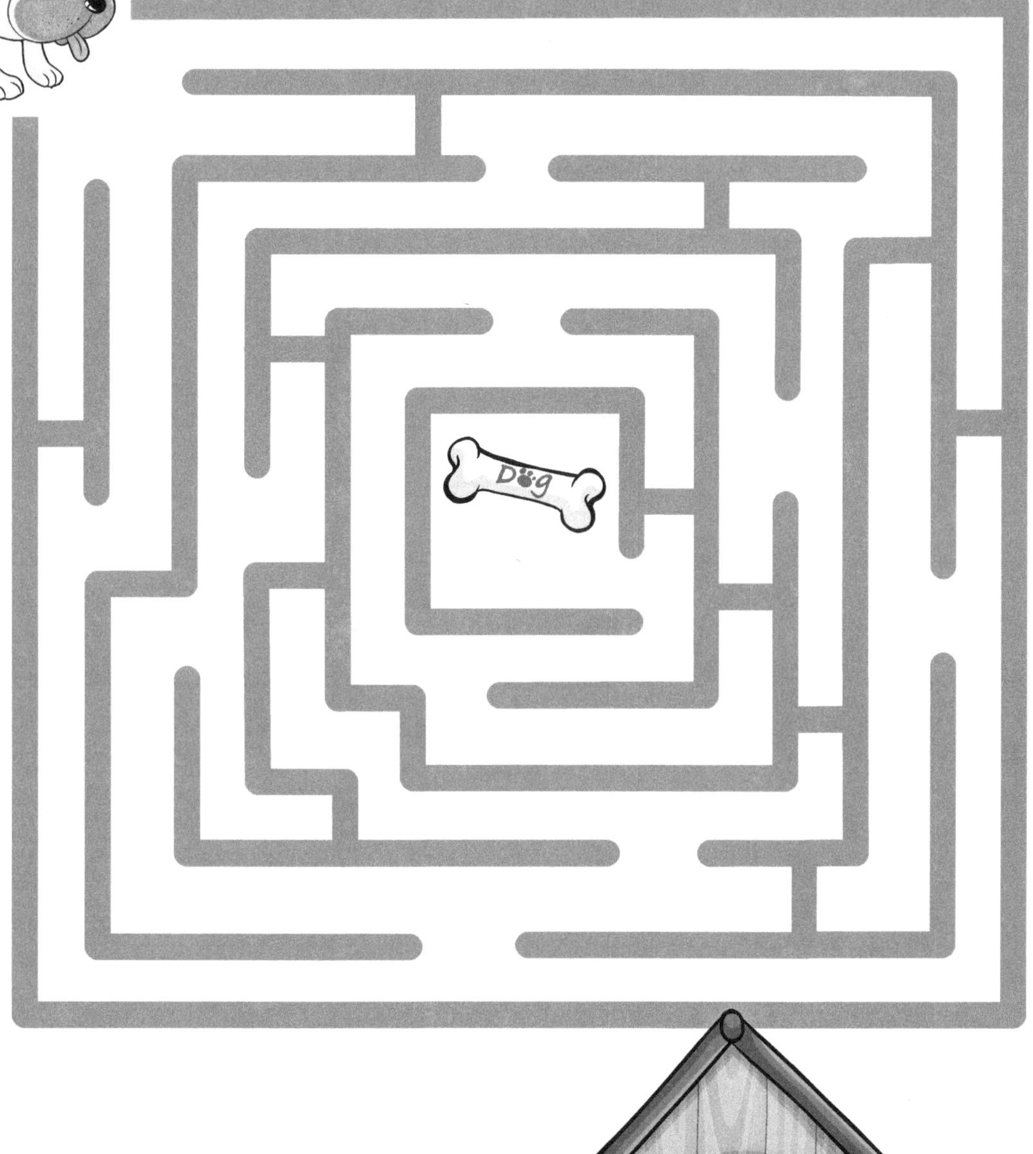

Directions: Help the dog find his way to the bone.

Directions: Say the colors' names. Then, color the umbrella.

Language Arts Activity

Have your child look through some books to find words that contain only letters that he or she has practiced writing, including: *a, b, c, d, e, f, g, h, i, j, k, l, m, n, o, p, q,* and *r.* Have your child make a list of those words.

Mathematics Activity

Give your child counters, such as beans, buttons, or O-shaped cereal. Have your child count seven counters. Then, separate the seven counters into two groups, such as six and one, two and five, or three and four. Have your child count each group and then the whole group of seven.

Social Studies Activity

Review page 107 with your child. Discuss other people he or she likes to help. Have your child draw a picture of him or her helping those people. Ask your child why he or she likes helping these people and how they help the community.

Critical-Thinking Activity

Have your child draw at least seven different shapes on a sheet of paper. Then, have your child draw a path through them like a maze. Have your child color his or her work of art and give it to a family member.

Listening-and-Speaking Activity

Ask your child to make up a funny story about how food gets to his or her dinner plate. Ask your child to tell you his or her story.

Directions: Trace.

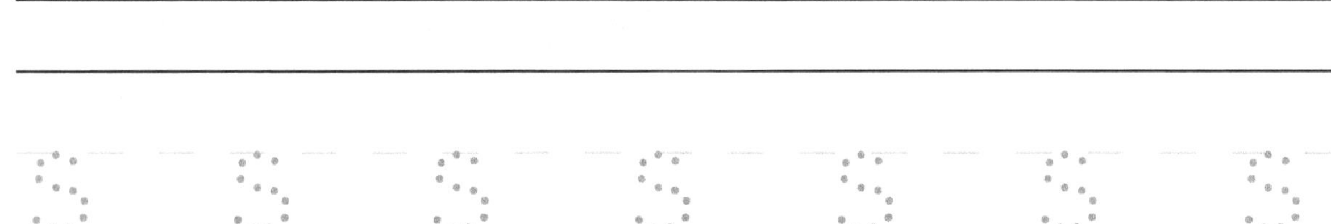

Directions: Write the letter Ss.

Directions: Say and trace.

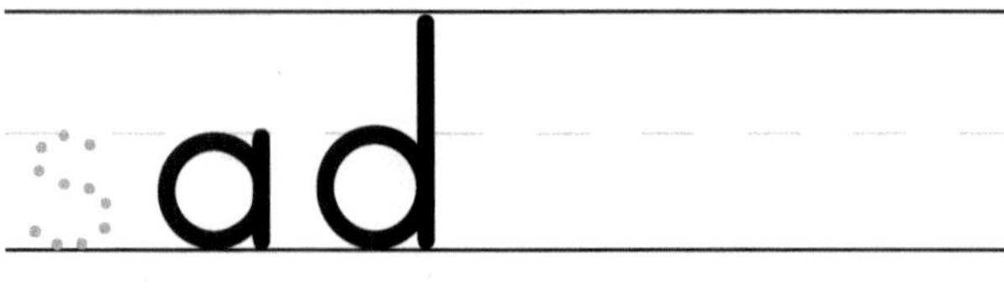

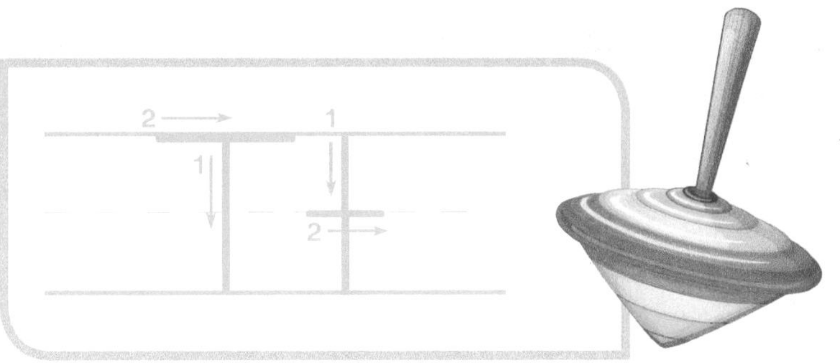

Directions: Trace.

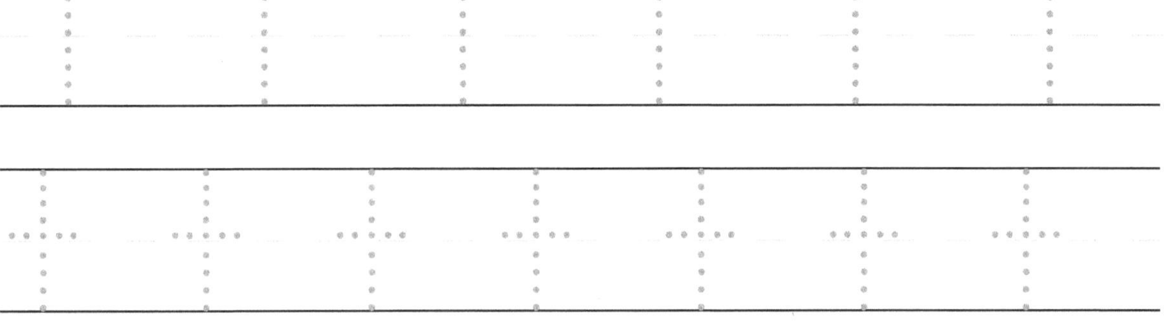

Directions: Write the letter Tt.

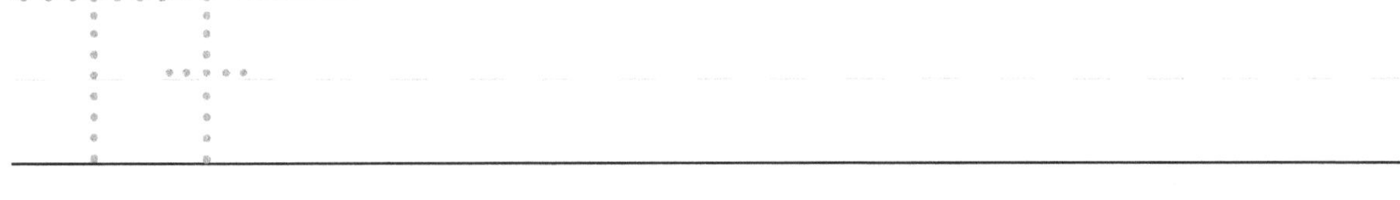

Directions: Say and trace.

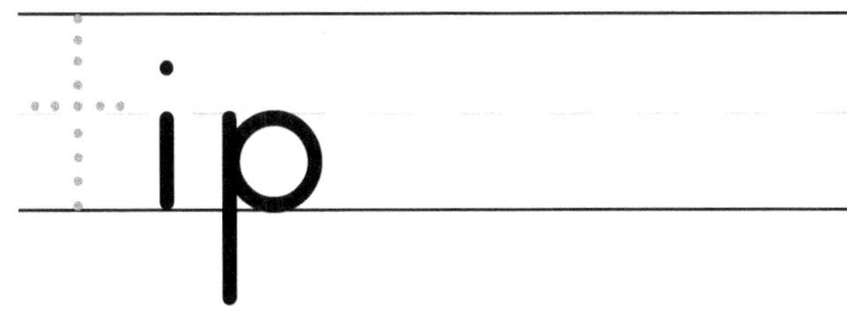

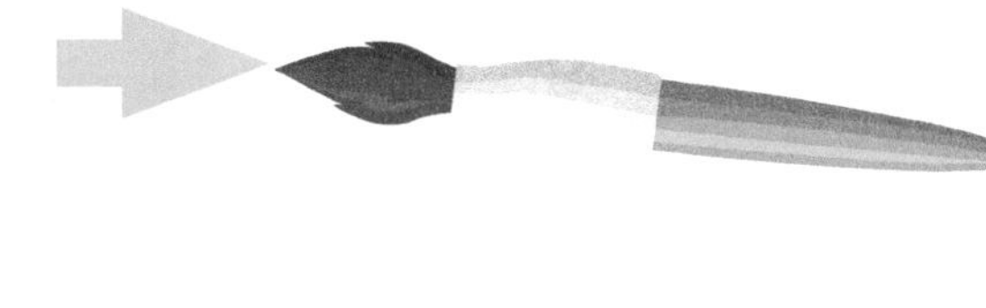

Directions: Trace.

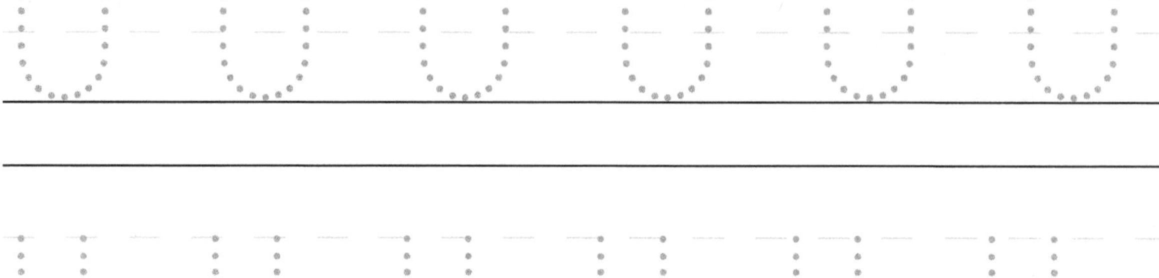

Directions: Write the letter Uu.

Directions: Say and trace.

mbrella

s n

u	s	u	t	u	s
T	T	S	U	T	S
U	S	U	T	U	T
t	s	t	u	s	t
s	t	s	u	s	u
S	S	T	U	S	T

Directions: Circle the letters that match the letter in the left column.

star

bus

tree

car

us

bee

Directions: Say the name of each picture. Draw lines to match the words that rhyme.

Directions: Draw your favorite weather. Write a label for your picture.

Directions: Trace.

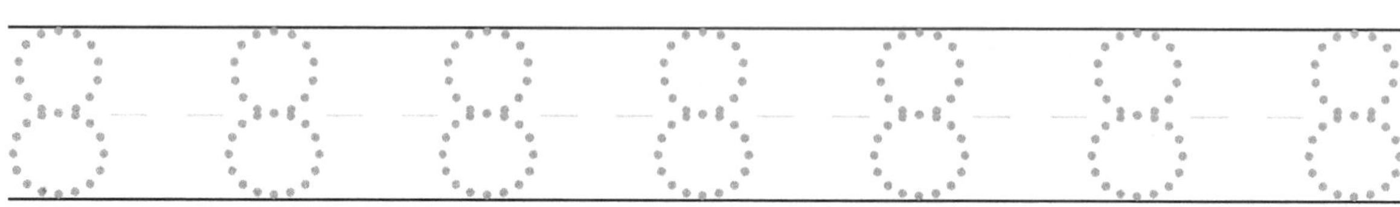

Directions: Write the number 8.

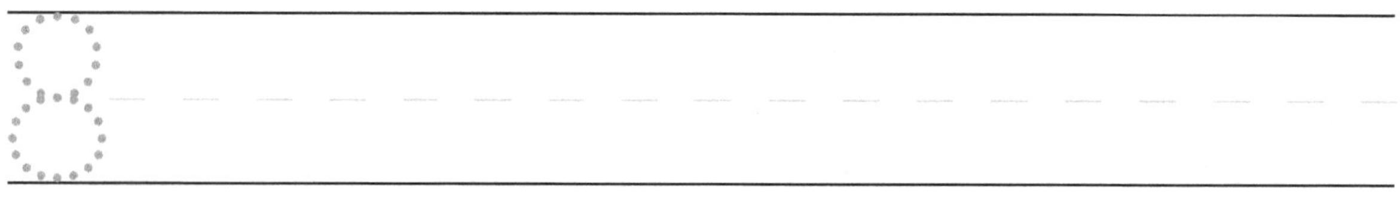

Directions: Say and trace.

I see 8 suns.

Directions: Look at each group of objects. Cross out the one that does not belong.

Directions: Count each group. Then, write the number of objects.

1 + 3 = ______

4 + 4 = ______

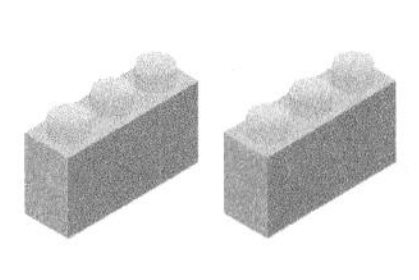 

2 + 4 = ______

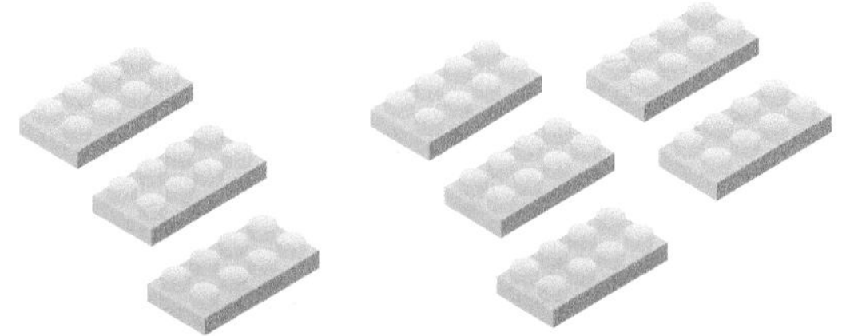

3 + 5 = ______

1 + 2 = ______

Directions: Add the objects.

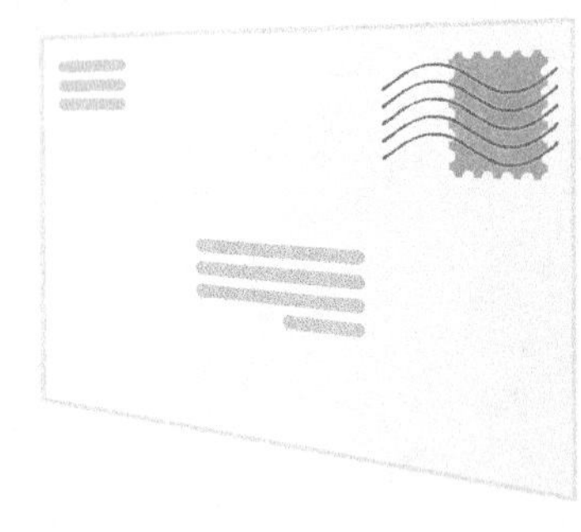

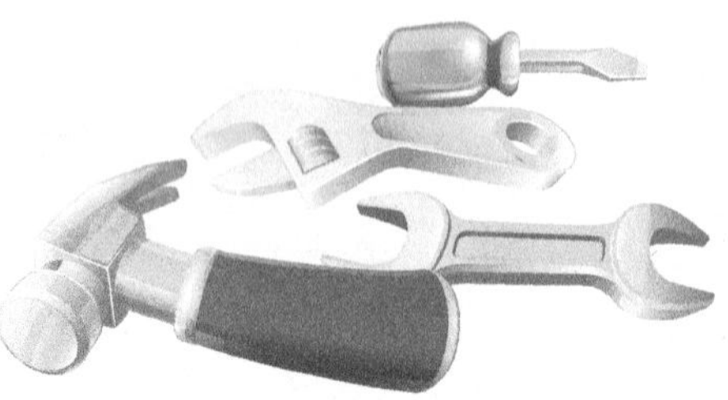

Directions: Look at the objects in both columns. Draw lines to show where the objects on the left belong.

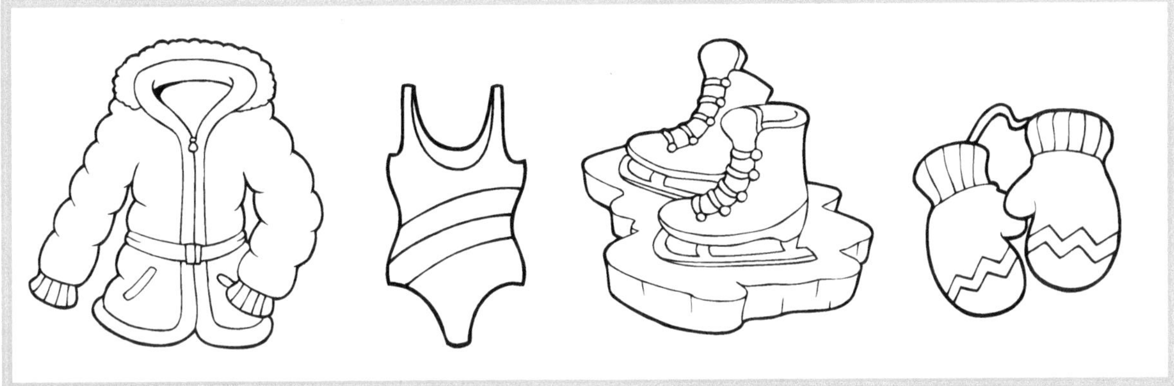

Directions: Name the objects in each row. Color the objects that go together in each row. Cross out the one that doesn't fit.

Directions: Color the items that are smaller than you. Cross out anything that is bigger than you.

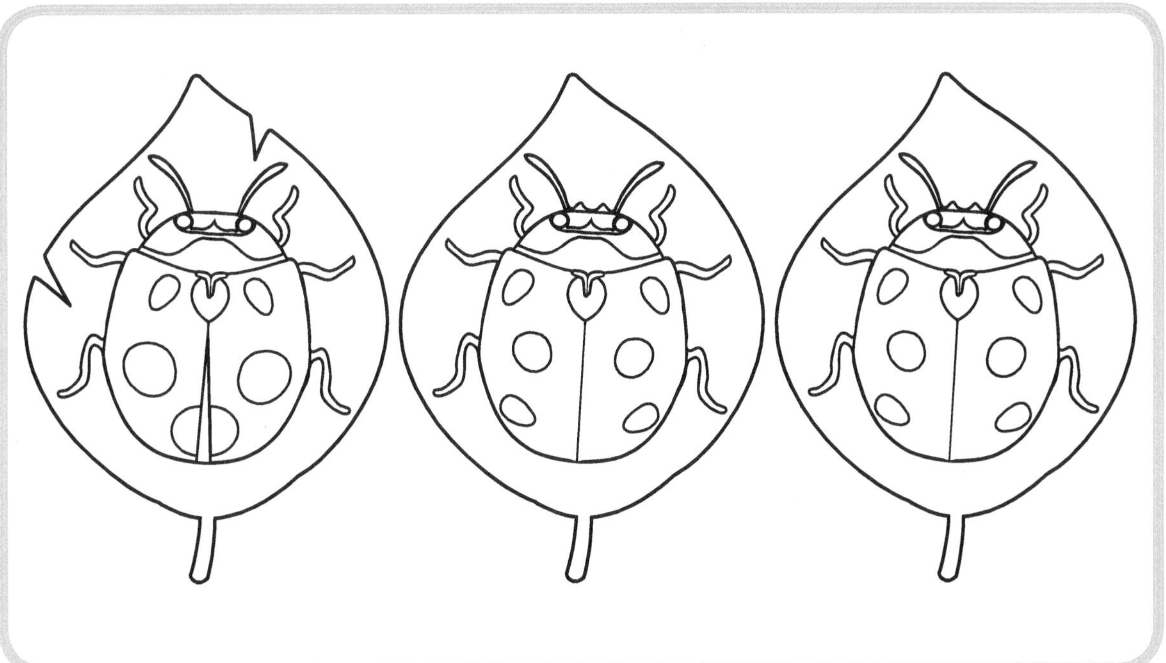

Directions: Look at the pictures. Color the matching pairs so they look exactly the same.

Language Arts Activity

Have your child write these words three times each: *sat, set, sit, tap, tip, top, sunset.*

Mathematics Activity

Have your child draw pictures to show these addition problems: 2 + 1; 3 + 1; 1 + 4.

Science Activity

Ask your child what his or her favorite season is. Have your child draw a picture of himself or herself playing outside during that season. Tell your child to include details that show the weather.

Critical-Thinking Activity

Have your child draw a picture showing at least two animals. Tell your child to include at least two silly things in the picture. Have your child give the picture to a friend or family member to see whether that person can find the silly things.

Listening-and-Speaking Activity

Ask your child to make up a story about his or her favorite animal. Then, have your child tell you his or her story. Ask your child questions about the story, such as *What is the animal's life like? What does it do? Why is it your favorite animal?*

Directions: Trace.

Directions: Write the letter Vv.

Directions: Say and trace.

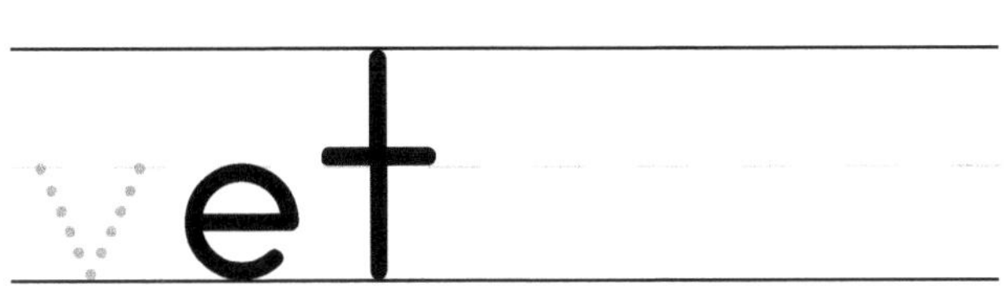

an

et

Directions: Trace.

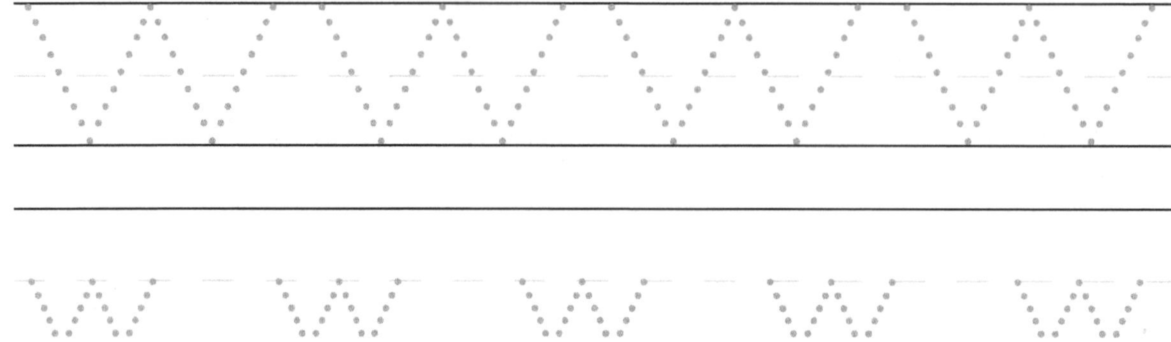

Directions: Write the letter Ww.

Directions: Say and trace.

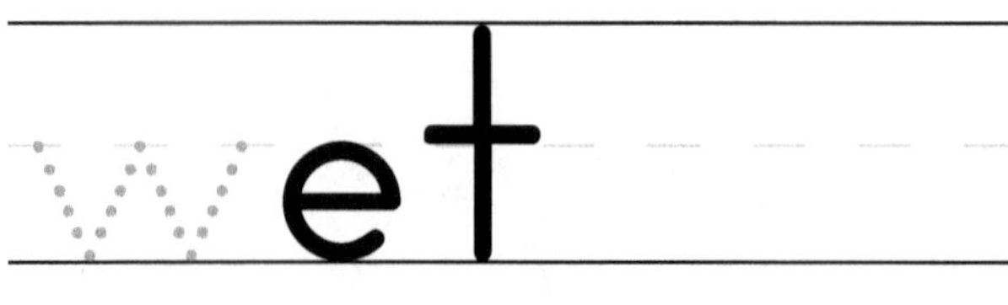

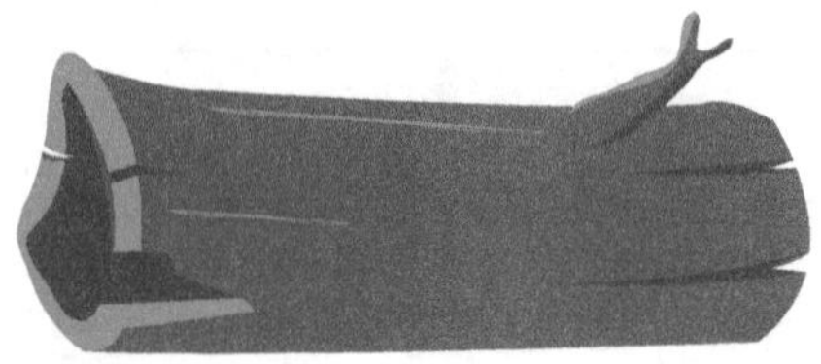

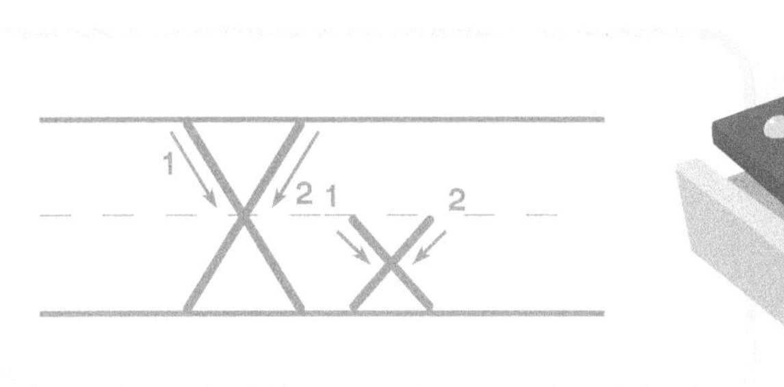

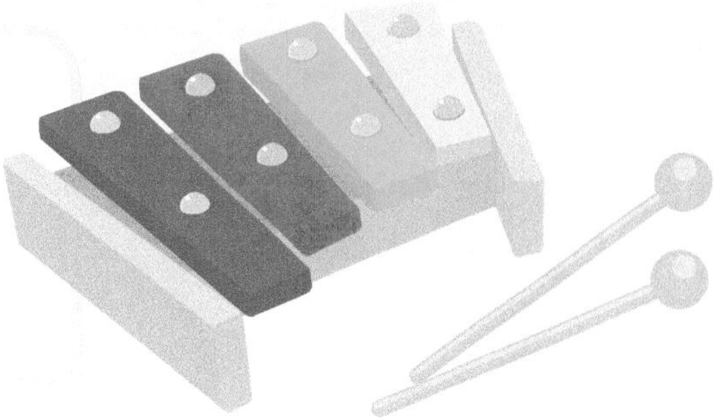

Directions: Trace.

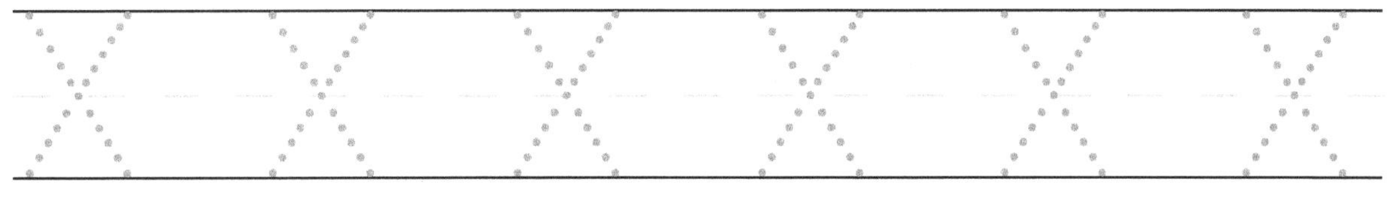

Directions: Write the letter Xx.

Directions: Say and trace.

a x e

e x i t

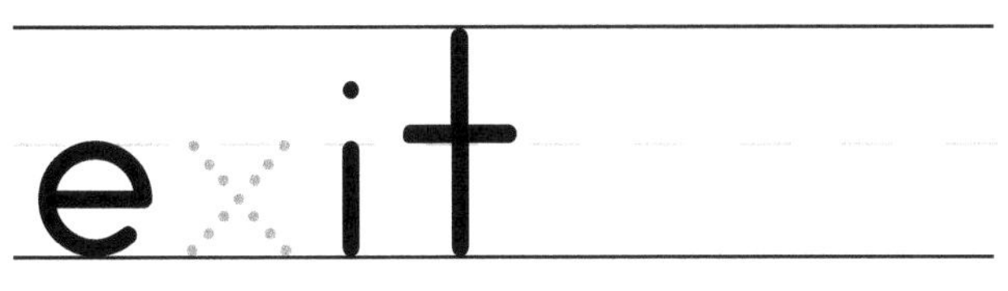

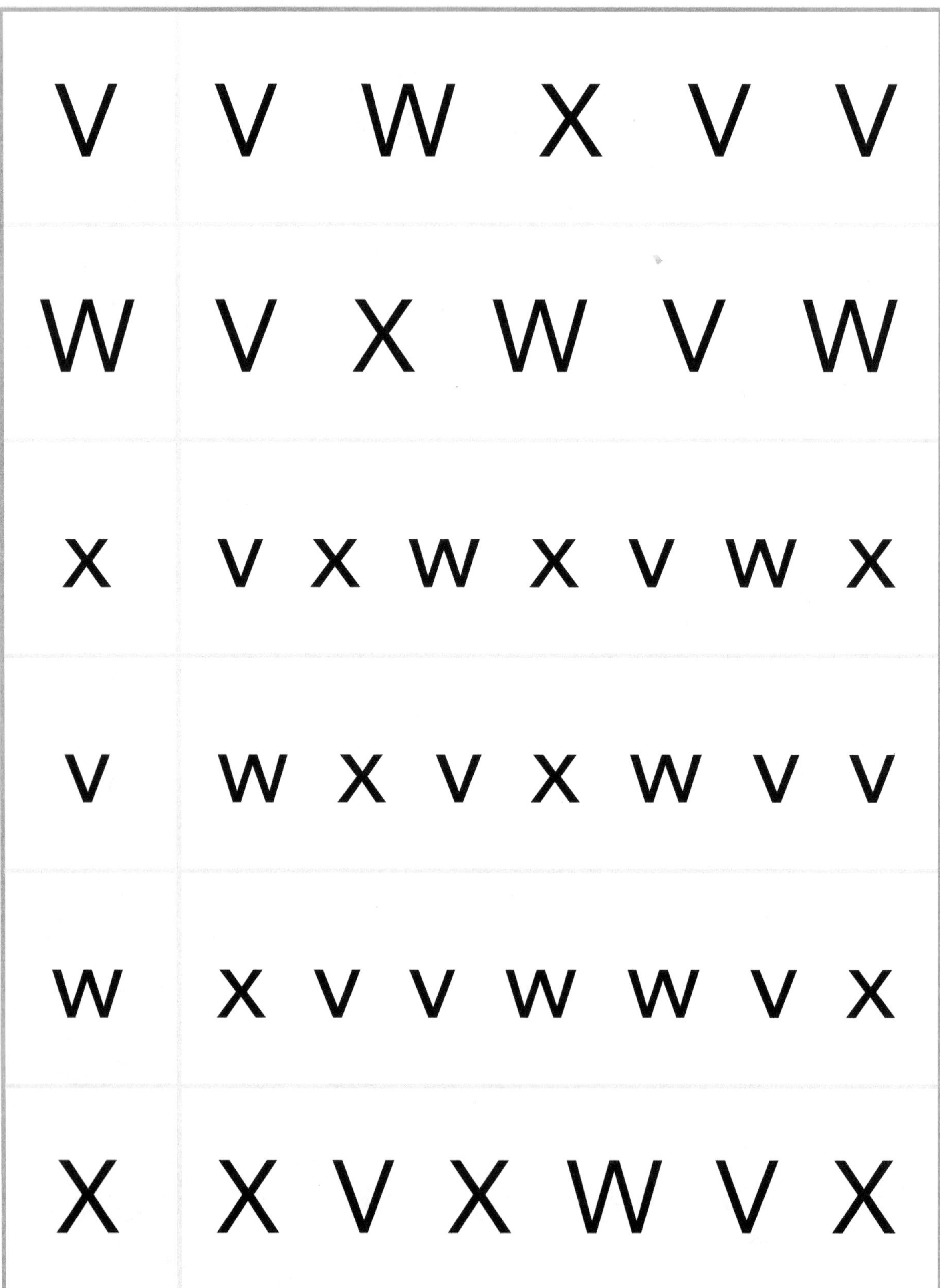

V	V W X V V
W	V X W V W
x	v x w x v w x
v	w x v x w v v
w	x v v w w v x
X	X V X W V X

Directions: Circle the letters that match the letter in the left column.

van

pail

whale

free

tree

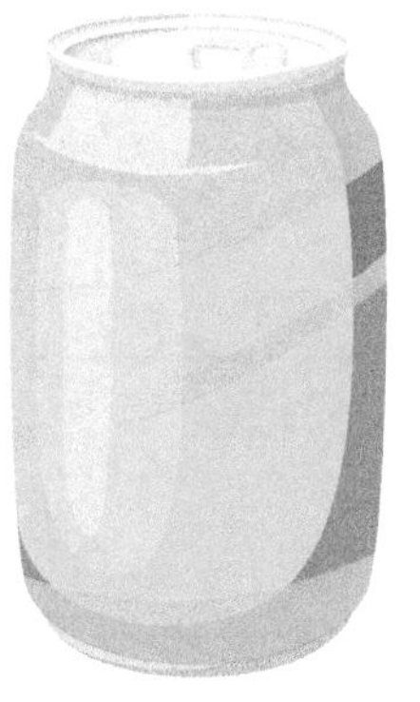

can

Directions: Say the name of each picture. Draw lines to match the words that rhyme.

Directions: Draw yourself in your favorite clothes. Write your full name.

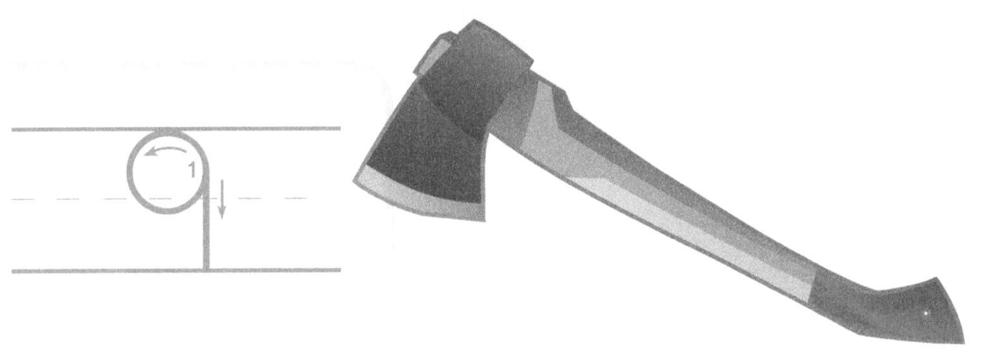

Directions: Trace.

Directions: Write the number 9.

Directions: Say and trace.

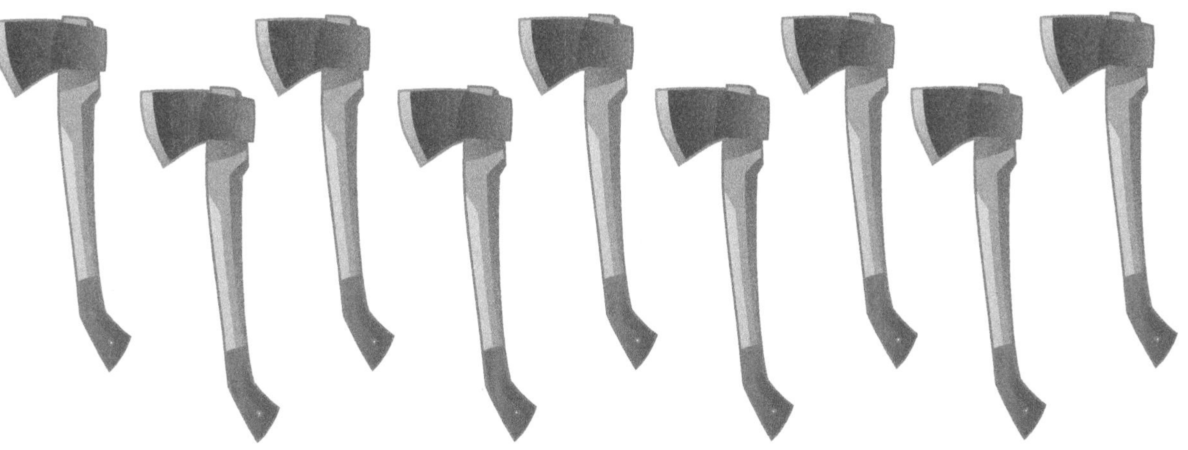

I see 9 axes.

Directions: Color the ◗ red, the ◇ blue, the ♡ green, and the ☆ yellow.

Directions: Draw 5 fish.

Directions: Draw 6 dogs.

Directions: Draw 9 people.

1 + 6 = ______

2 + 5 = ______

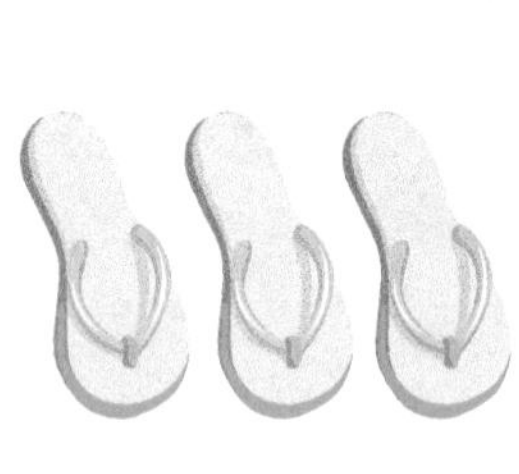

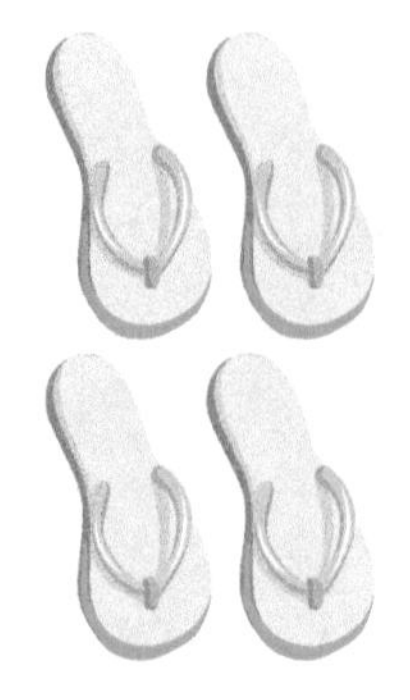

3 + 4 = ______

4 + 1 = ______

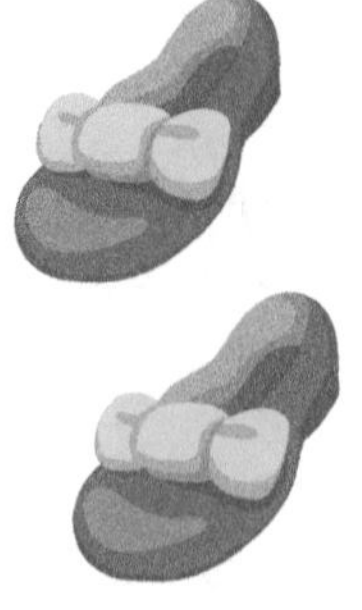

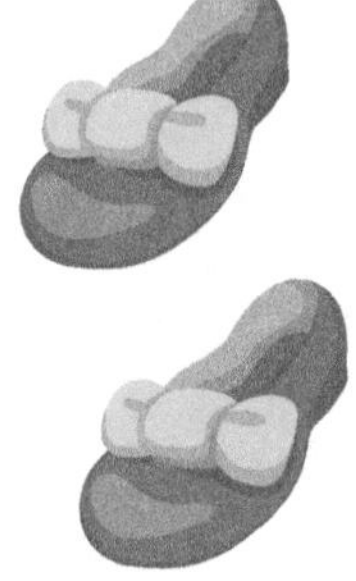

5 + 4 = ______

2 + 2 = ______

Directions: Add the objects.

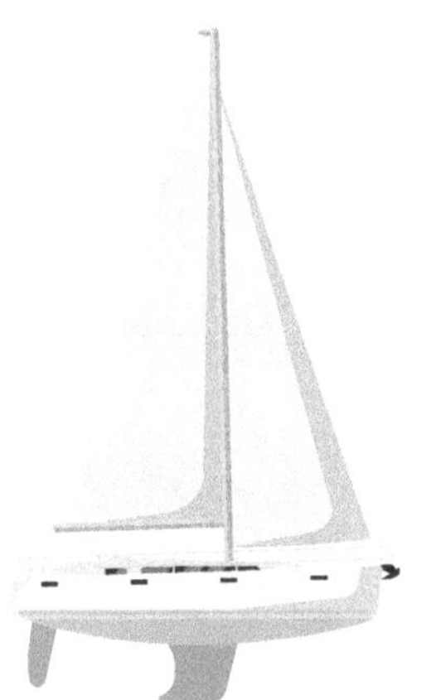

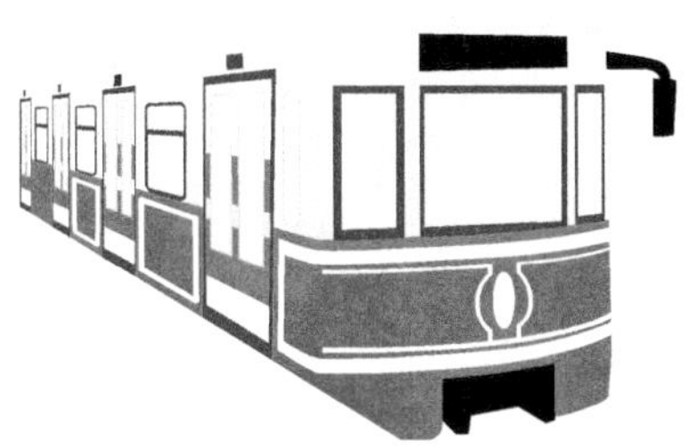

Directions: Look at the vehicles. Draw a line from each vehicle to where you would find it.

Directions: Number the pictures in order. Color the pictures.

Directions: Draw the next shape in each pattern.

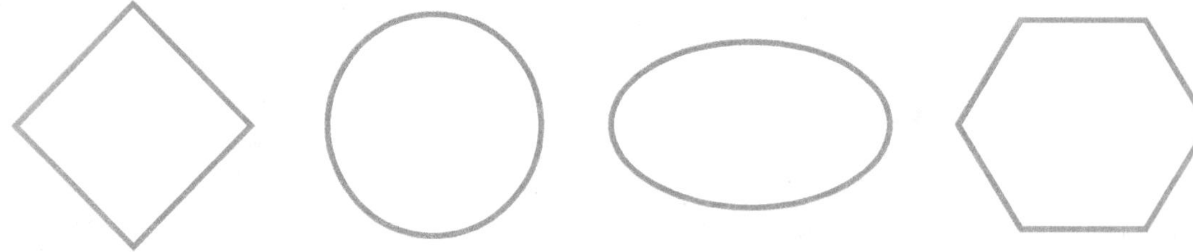

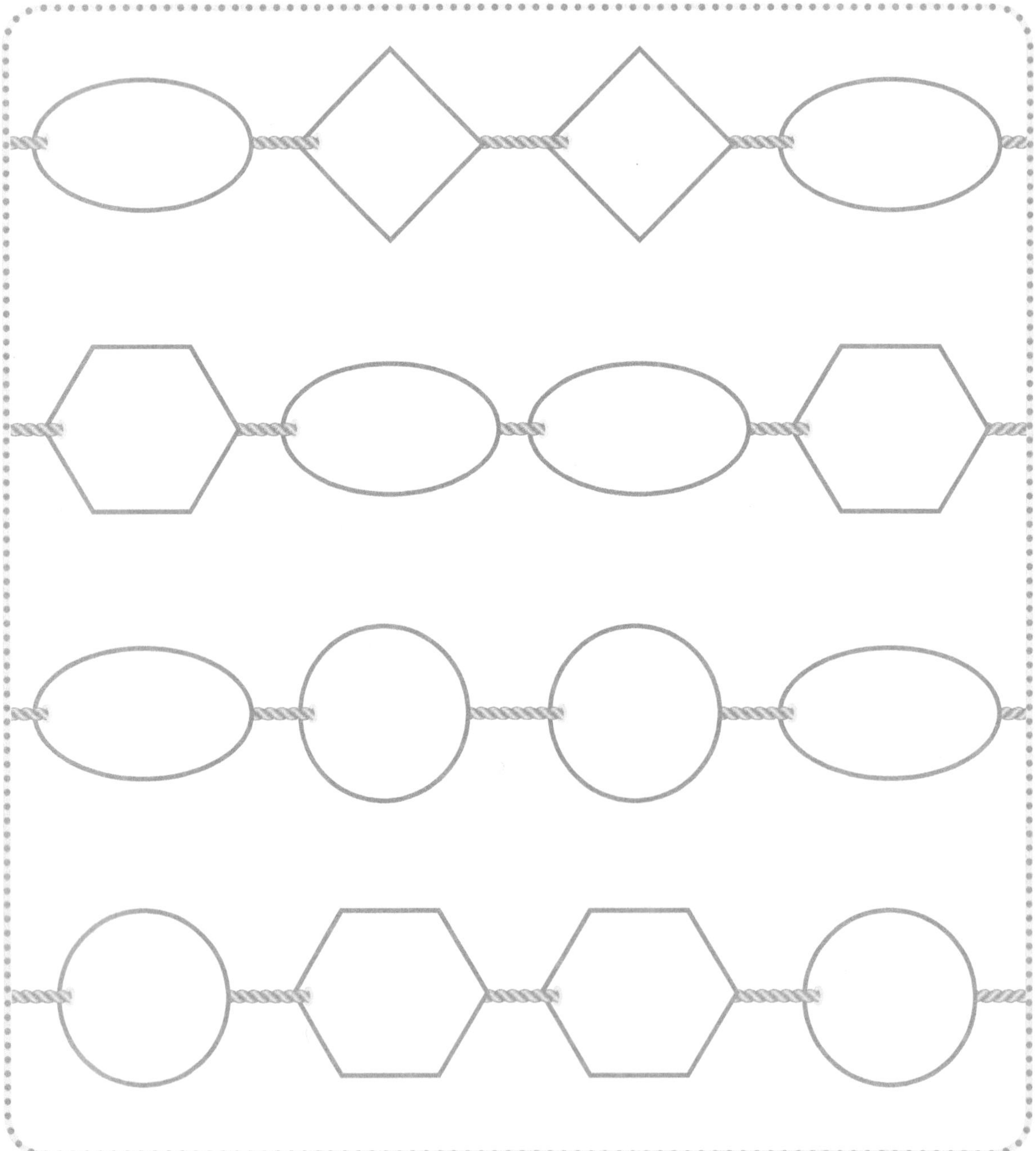

Directions: Color the shapes at the top of the page. Use that as a guide to color the rest of the shapes on the page.

Language Arts Activity

Tell your child that there are only two letters left in the alphabet. Ask him or her what they are. Have your child say as many words that start with *Y* and *Z* as he or she can. Challenge your child to list at least 10 words.

Mathematics Activity

Have your child write as many different ways to make 9 as he or she can, such as 1 + 8.

Social Studies Activity

Ask your child to think of a vehicle he or she sees around the community. Have your child draw a picture of it and label two parts on the vehicle. Ask your child what is special about this vehicle.

Critical-Thinking Activity

Have your child draw three patterns using different shapes and colors. Have your child give his or her patterns to a friend or family member and ask that person to draw the next shapes in the patterns.

Listening-and-Speaking Activity

Ask your child to make up a story about how a plant grows. Tell your child to imagine that he or she is the plant and that he or she should talk about life as a plant. Then, ask your child to tell you his or her story.

Directions: Trace.

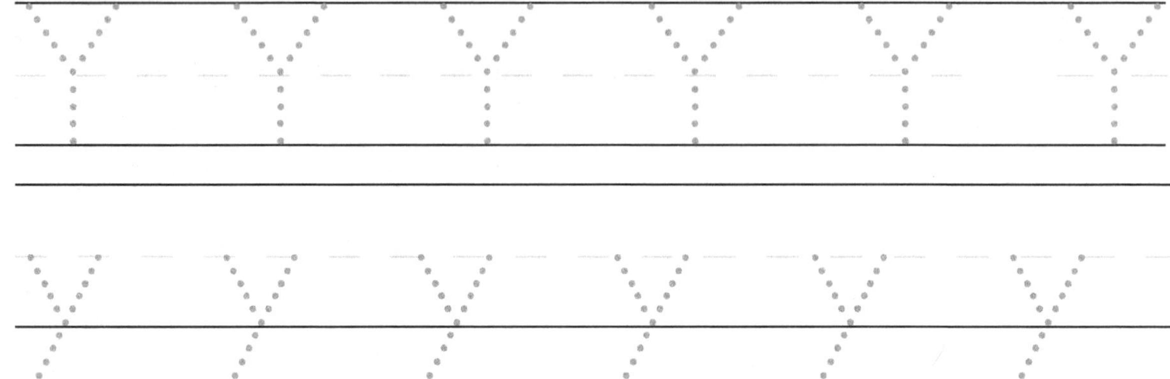

Directions: Write the letter Yy.

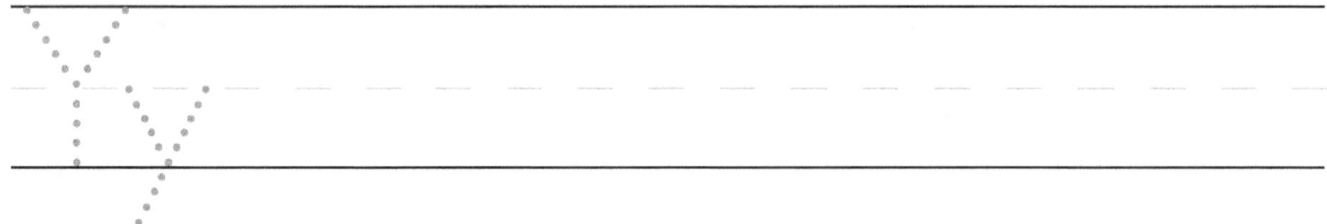

Directions: Say and trace.

eye

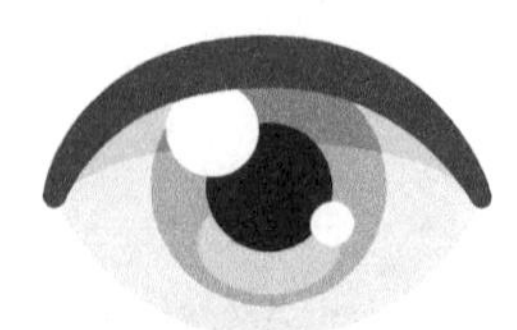

yes

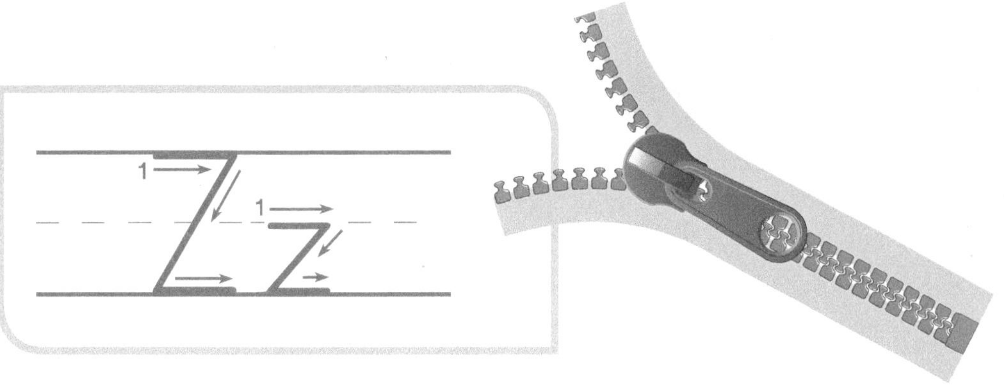

Directions: Trace.

Directions: Write the letter Zz.

Directions: Say and trace.

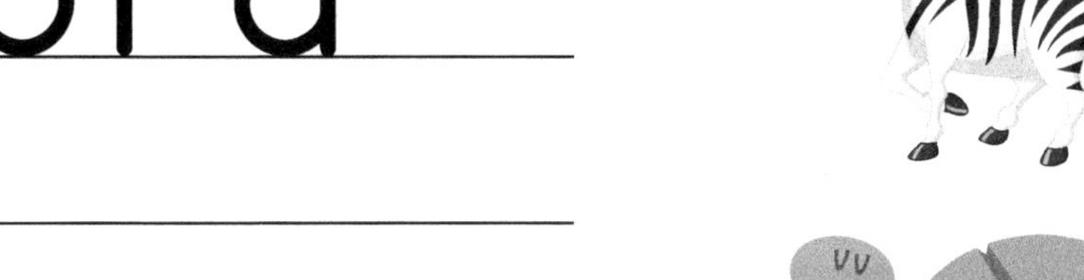

ebra

oo

A	P
S	C
K	D
E	H
B	Z

Directions: Fill in the missing parts. Make the letters in each box match.

Directions: Circle the letters hidden in the room. Then, color the picture.

Directions: Circle the picture that matches each ending sound.

Directions: Draw yourself in your room. Write a word to describe your room.

Directions: Trace.

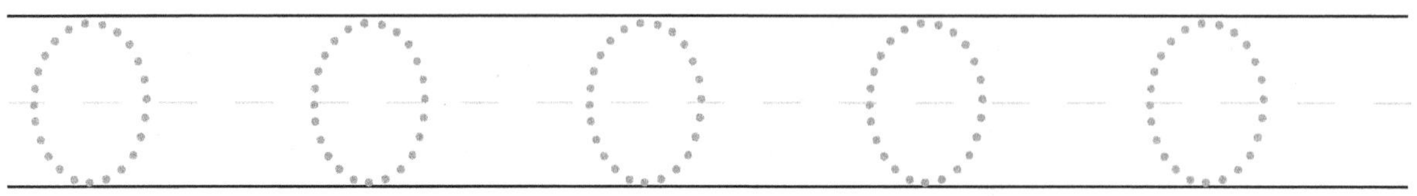

Directions: Write the number 0.

Directions: Say and trace.

I see 0 yo-yos.

Direction: Find and color the triangles, squares, circles, and rectangles.

Directions: Draw 8 circles. ○

Directions: Draw 10 squares. □

Directions: Draw 9 stars. ☆

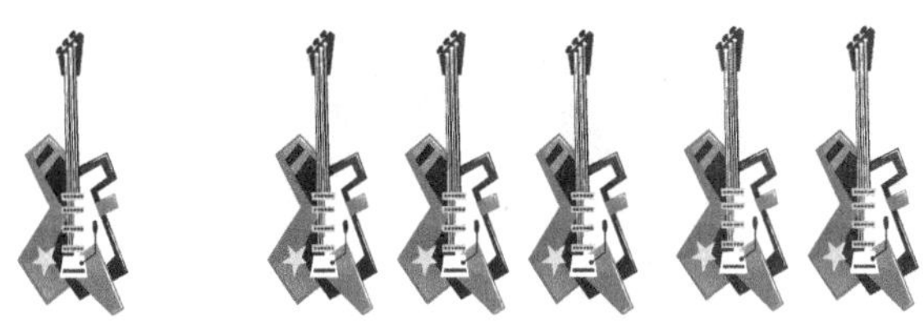

9 + 0 = ________

1 + 5 = ________

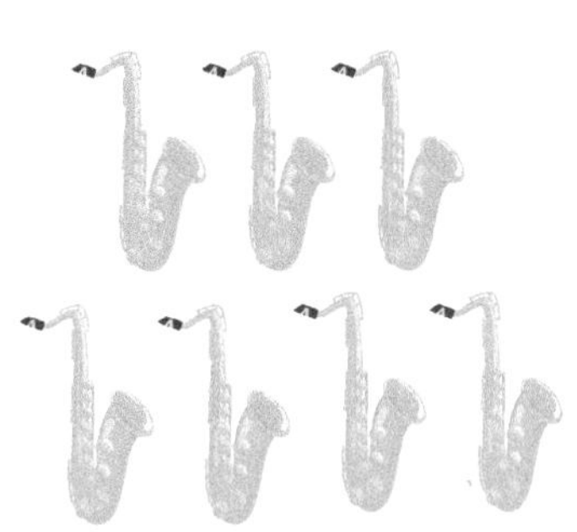

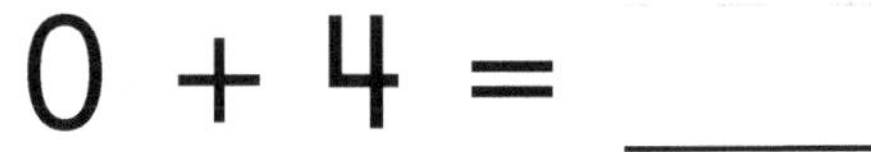

0 + 4 = ________

7 + 1 = ________

5 + 0 = ________

3 + 2 = ________

Directions: Add the objects.

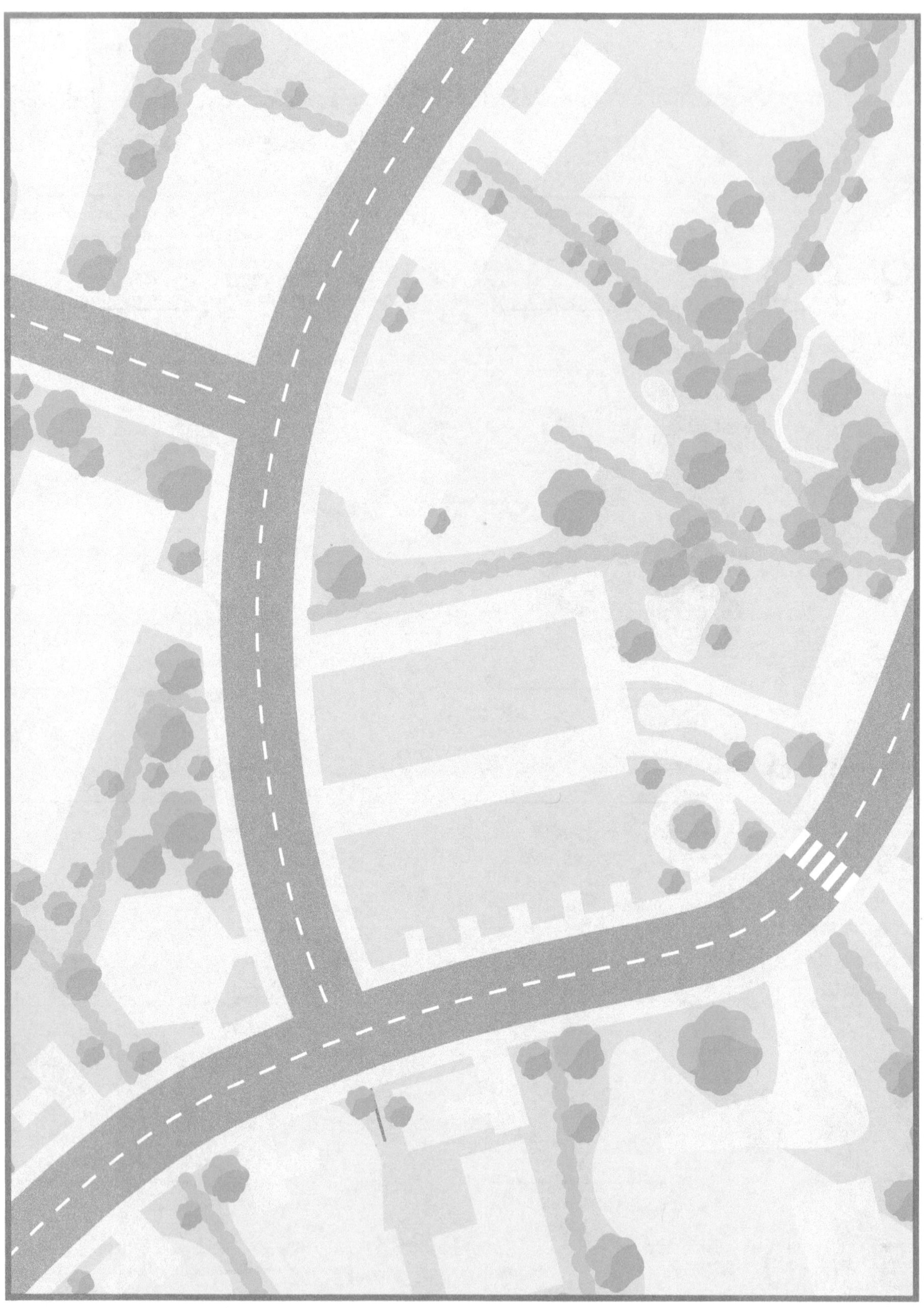

Directions: Add these to the map. Add a house. Add a school. Add a store. Add a car.

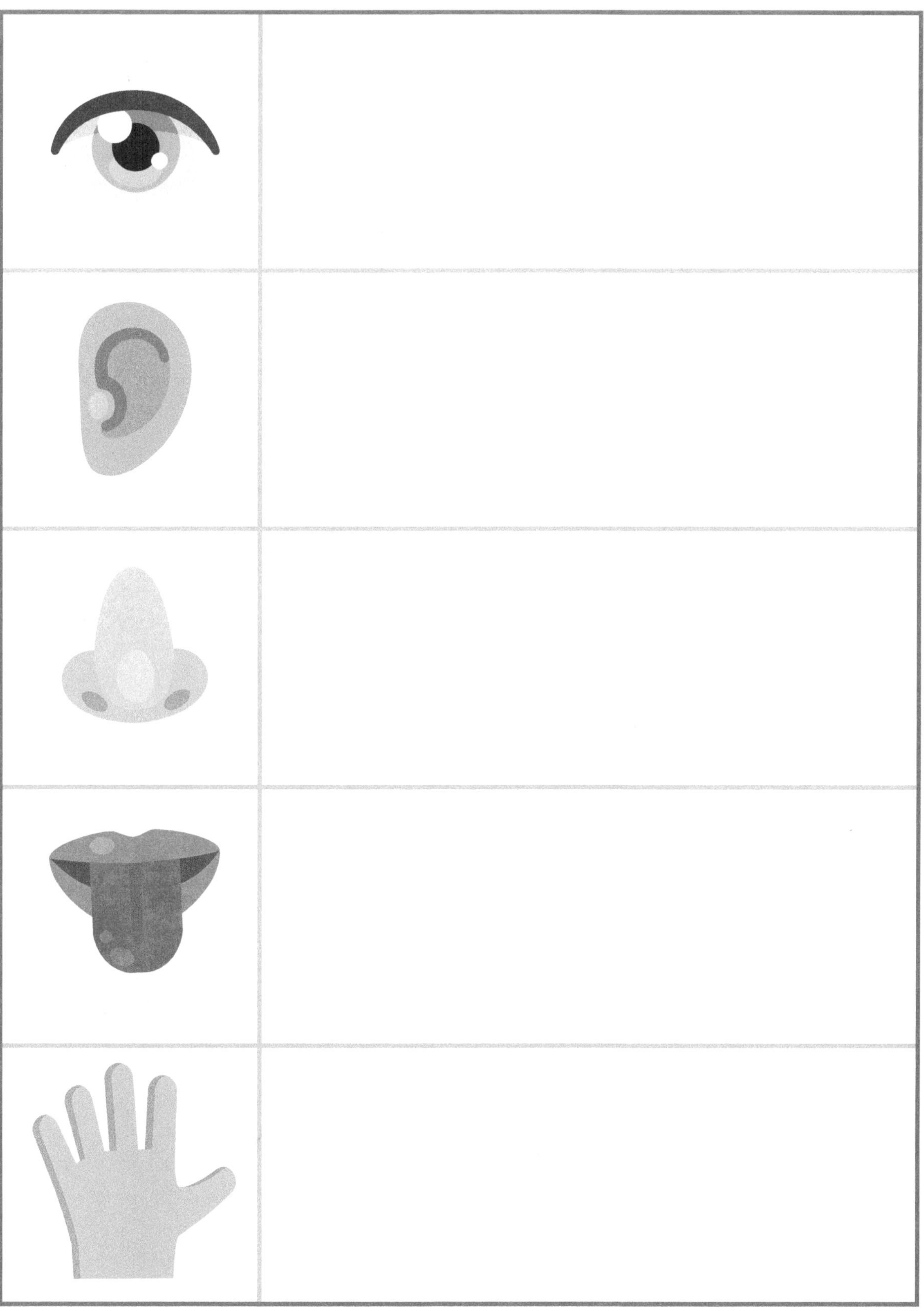

Directions: Draw pictures of things you can see, hear, smell, taste, and touch.

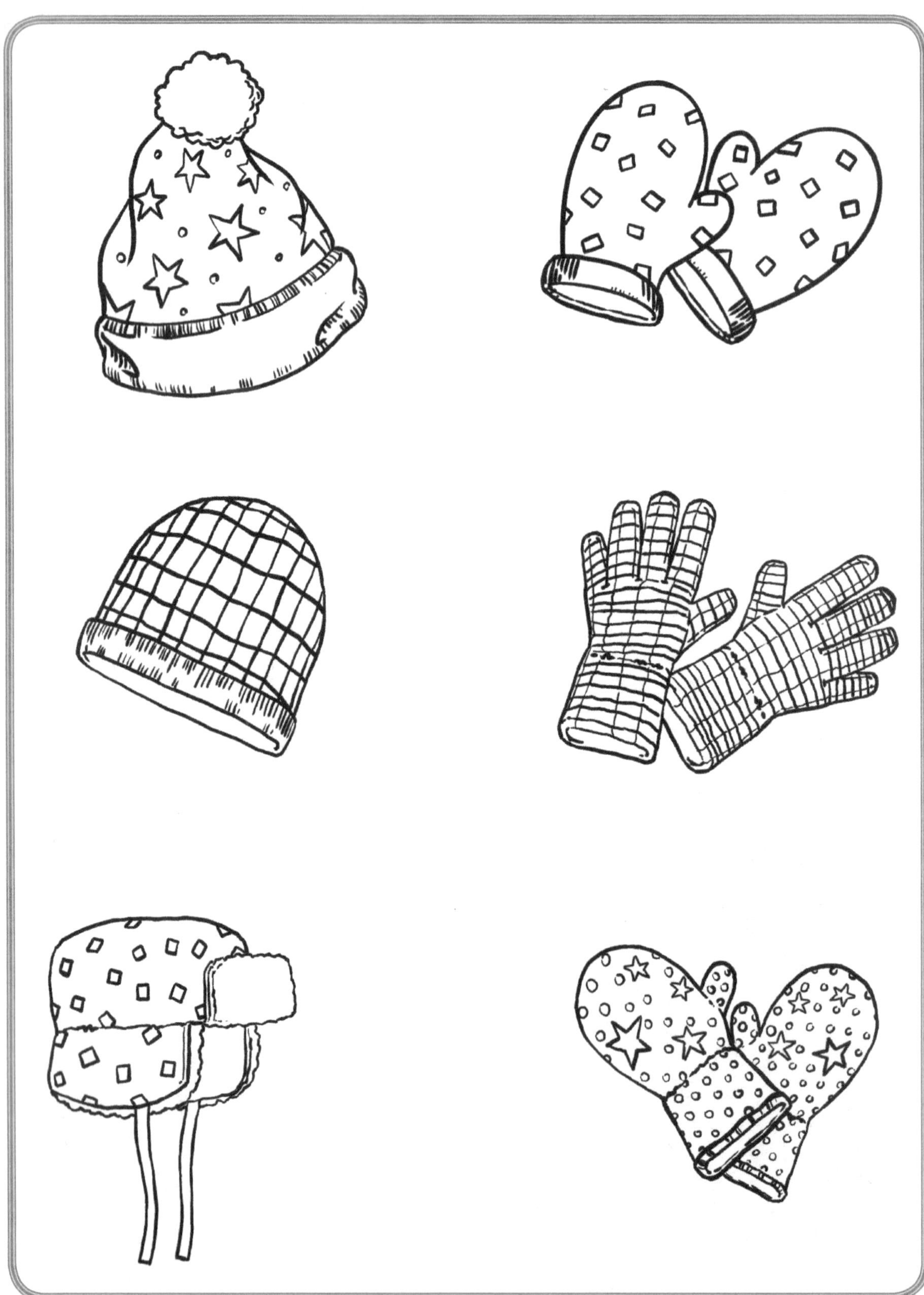

Directions: Draw a line to connect each hat with the matching mittens. Then, color the pictures.

1–blue
2–orange
3–yellow
4–green
5–red
6–purple
7–brown

Directions: Color in each part of the picture.

Language Arts Activity

Have your child write the whole alphabet in order. Have your child use this book to help him or her write the letters in the correct order.

Mathematics Activity

Have your child write four original addition problems. Have your child give them to a friend or a family member to solve.

Social Studies Activity

Review the map on page 152 with your child. Point out the roads. Have your child trace them with his or her finger. Then, discuss objects that are near each other on the map.

Science Activity

Ask your child which sense is his or her favorite. Then, have your child draw a picture of himself or herself using that sense.

Critical-Thinking Activity

Challenge your child to draw a picture using only his or her favorite color. Ask your child how he or she can make the picture interesting.

Listening-and-Speaking Activity

Ask your child to make up a story about what life would be like if he or she could not use one of his or her senses. Ask your child to tell you his or her story.

Answer Key

There are many open-ended pages, problems, and pictures in this book. For those activities, the answers will vary. Answers are only given in this answer key if they are specific.

page 7

Check that the lines are traced reasonably well.

page 8

Check that the lines and circles are traced reasonably well.

page 9

Check that the lines are traced reasonably well.

page 10

Check that the lines are traced reasonably well.

page 11

Check that the student correctly identifies the beginning sounds.

page 13

Check that the numbers are traced and written reasonably well.

page 14

Check that the circles are traced reasonably well.

page 15

one bear—one pig

two toads—two fish

three lions—three rabbits

page 16

The larger item in each set should be colored.

page 18

Pictures should include an umbrella, boots, and a coat. Check that the word *rain* is traced reasonably well.

page 19

Top-left: 4

Top-right: 2

Bottom-left: 3

Bottom-right: 1

page 20

The apple, strawberry, stop sign, rose, and cherry should be colored.

page 22

Check that the letters are traced and written reasonably well.

page 23

Check that the letters are traced and written reasonably well.

page 24

Check that the letters are traced and written reasonably well.

page 25

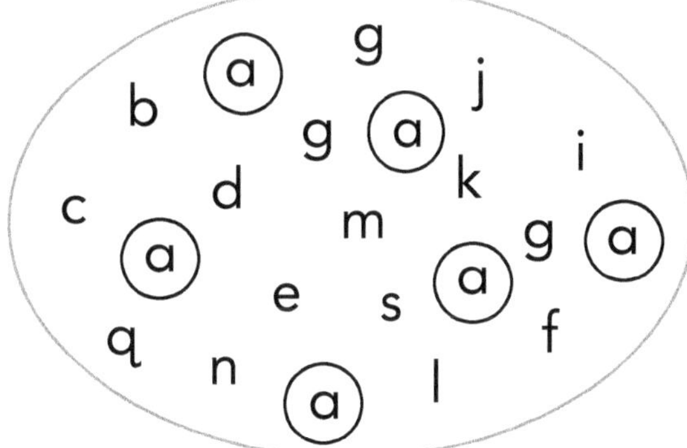

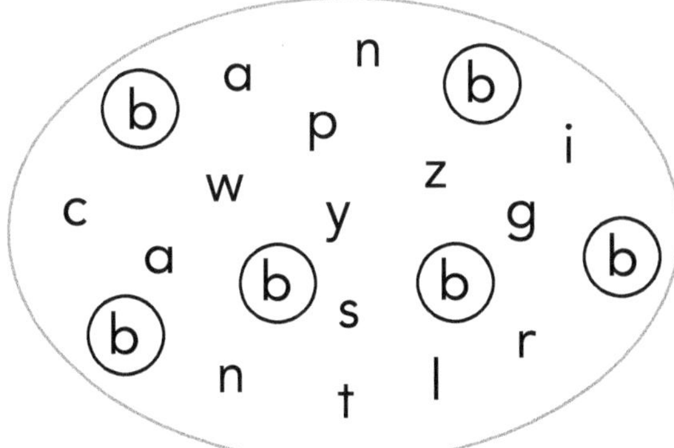

page 26

A—apple

B—bird

C—cat

page 28

Check that the numbers are traced and written reasonably well.

page 29

Check that the squares are traced reasonably well.

page 30

1 ball

2 carrots

1 banana

2 apples

page 31

The five large shoes should be colored, and the rest should be circled.

page 33

cow—the third image should be circled.

duck—the first image should be circled.

sheep—the third image should be circled.

horse—the second image should be circled.

goat—the third image should be circled.

goose—the second image should be circled.

page 34

monkey—bananas

rabbit—carrot

mouse—cheese

dog—bone

bear—honey

page 35

The whale, pants, berries, and bird should be colored.

page 37

Check that the letters are traced and written reasonably well.

page 38

Check that the letters are traced and written reasonably well.

page 39

Check that the letters are traced and written reasonably well.

page 40

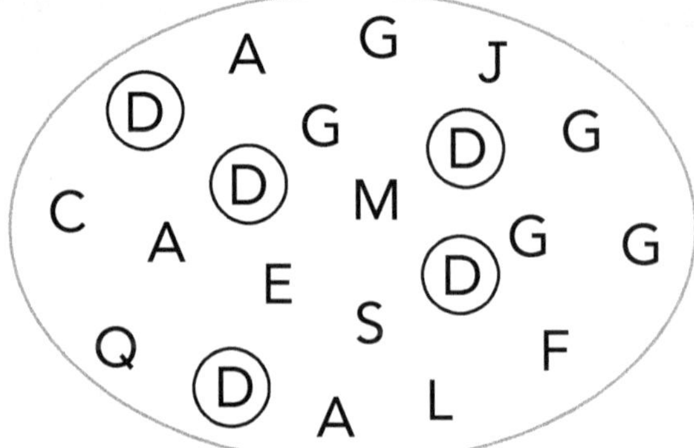

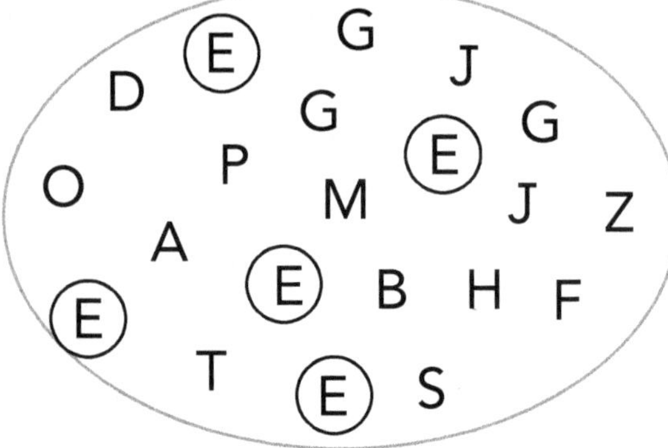

page 41

D—dog

E—elephant

F—fox

page 43

Check that the numbers are traced and written reasonably well.

page 44

Check that the triangles are traced reasonably well.

page 44

Check that the triangles are traced reasonably well.

page 45

3 apples

1 book

2 pencils

3 bones

page 46

The first heart should be colored red, the second one should be circled, and the third one should be colored blue.

The first butterfly should be colored blue, the second one should be circled, and the third one should be colored red.

The first fish should be circled, the second one should be colored red, and the third one should be colored blue.

The first star should be colored blue, the second one should be circled, and the third one should be colored red.

The first gem should be colored red, the second one should be circled, and the third one should be colored blue.

page 47

crayons—crayon box

lunch—lunch bag

book—bookcase

paintbrush—easel

page 48

The sun, fire, and candle should be circled.

The snowman, ice, and ice cream should be crossed out.

page 49

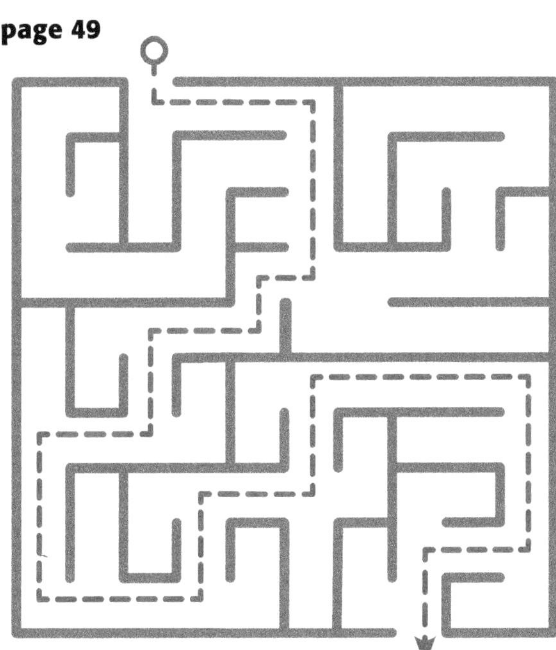

page 50

The banana, sun, taxi, sunflower, and corn should be colored yellow.

page 52

Check that the letters are traced and written reasonably well.

page 53

Check that the letters are traced and written reasonably well.

page 54

Check that the letters are traced and written reasonably well.

page 55

Check that capital letters are matched with the correct lowercase letters.

page 56

hat—h

hand—h

igloo—i

goat—g

grapes—g

house—h

ice—i

ice cream—i

glue—g

page 58

Check that the numbers are traced and written reasonably well.

page 59

Check that the rectangles are traced reasonably well.

page 60

Check that the correct shapes are drawn in the given amounts.

page 61

On the left, a flower should be drawn that is shorter than the given flower. On the right, a flower should be drawn that is taller than the given flower.

The mama bear should be shorter than the given bear. The baby bear should be shorter than the mama bear.

page 63

The scarf, ice skates, snowflake, coat, and snowman should be colored blue.

The shorts, ball, sandals, shovel and pail, and swimming pool should be colored yellow.

page 64

The third fish should be circled.

The first ball should be circled.

The second tree should be circled.

The third pizza slice should be circled.

page 65

The frog, leaves, peas, and iguana should be colored green.

page 67

Check that the letters are traced and written reasonably well.

page 68

Check that the letters are traced and written reasonably well.

page 69

Check that the letters are traced and written reasonably well.

page 70

Check that the capital letters are matched with the correct lowercase letters.

page 71

lion—l

kite—k

jar—j

lollipop—l

jellyfish—j

leaf—l

koala—k

jump—j

key—k

page 73

Check that the numbers are traced and written reasonably well.

page 74

Check that all four circles are colored blue, all three triangles are colored green, and all three rectangles are colored red.

page 75

Check that the correct shapes are drawn in the given amounts.

page 76

Check that the given number of pennies is circled in each row.

page 78

bird—nest

bee—beehive

cat—cat tower

snail—grass

dog—doghouse

page 79

teacher—board

mechanic—car

judge—gavel

firefighter—fire hydrant

page 80

The orange, carrot, basketball, pumpkin, and traffic cone should be colored.

page 82

Check that the letters are traced and written reasonably well.

page 83

Check that the letters are traced and written reasonably well.

page 84

Check that the letters are traced and written reasonably well.

page 85

All the letters that match the given letter on the left should be circled in each row.

page 86

M—mail

N—net

O—octopus

page 88

Check that the numbers are traced and written reasonably well.

page 89

Check that all three squares are colored yellow, all four circles are colored green, and all three triangles are colored blue.

page 90

Check that the drawing contains six circles, five squares, four triangles, and three rectangles.

page 91

Check that lines connect equal groups of nickels.

page 94

The glasses, pencil, strawberry, and scissors should be circled.

page 95

The plum, grapes, and flower should be colored. Check that all six colors are used in the rainbow.

page 97

Check that the letters are traced and written reasonably well.

page 98

Check that the letters are traced and written reasonably well.

page 99

Check that the letters are traced and written reasonably well.

page 100

All the letters that match the given letter on the left should be circled in each row.

page 101

P—pizza

Q—queen

R—rose

page 103

Check that the numbers are traced and written reasonably well.

page 104

Check that the shapes are traced reasonably well. Each row should be colored in a pattern.

page 105

5 sweaters

2 ducks

7 pencils

3 carrots

page 106

$2 + 1 = 3$

$3 + 2 = 5$

$5 + 1 = 6$

$2 + 2 = 4$

page 108

First row: 3, 2, 1

Second row: 1, 3, 2

Third row: 3, 1, 2

page 109

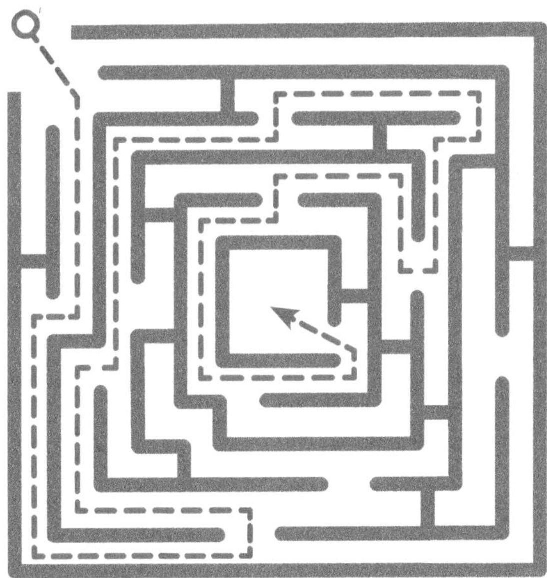

page 110

Check that each section of the umbrella is colored the correct color.

page 112

Check that the letters are traced and written reasonably well.

page 113

Check that the letters are traced and written reasonably well.

page 114

Check that the letters are traced and written reasonably well.

page 115

All the letters that match the given letter on the left should be circled in each row.

page 116

star–car

tree–bee

us–bus

page 118

Check that the numbers are traced and written reasonably well.

page 119

Top-left: The circle should be crossed out.

Top-right: The triangle should be crossed out.

Bottom-left: The star should be crossed out.

Bottom-right: The square should be crossed out.

page 120

5 balls

4 guitars

8 socks

6 blocks

page 121

$1 + 3 = 4$

$2 + 4 = 6$

$4 + 4 = 8$

$3 + 5 = 8$

$1 + 2 = 3$

page 122

envelope–mailbox

tools–toolbox

plant–pot

school supplies–backpack

page 123

Row 1: The ball should be crossed out, and the rest should be colored.

Row 2: The swimsuit should be crossed out, and the rest should be colored.

Row 3: The sled should be crossed out, and the rest should be colored.

Row 4: The umbrella should be crossed out, and the rest should be colored.

page 124

The chair, whale, and elephant should be crossed out. All others should be colored.

page 125

Check that the second and third ladybugs are colored exactly the same.

Check that the first and third cats are colored exactly the same.

page 127

Check that the letters are traced and written reasonably well.

page 128

Check that the letters are traced and written reasonably well.

page 129

Check that the letters are traced and written reasonably well.

page 130

All the letters that match the given letter on the left should be circled in each row.

page 131

van–can

whale–pail

tree–free

page 133

Check that the numbers are traced and written reasonably well.

page 134

Check that the semicircles are colored red, the diamonds are colored blue, the hearts are colored green, and the stars are colored yellow.

page 135

Check that the correct objects are drawn in the given amounts.

page 136

1 + 6 = 7

3 + 4 = 7

5 + 4 = 9

2 + 5 = 7

4 + 1 = 5

2 + 2 = 4

page 137

car—road

plane—sky

boat—water

train—rails

page 138

Top-left: 4

Top-right: 2

Bottom-left: 1

Bottom-right: 3

page 139

Row 1: triangle

Row 2: oval

Row 3: circle

Row 4: triangle

Row 5: heart

Row 6: semicircle

page 140

Check that the colors used to color the top shapes are used for the same shapes in each row.

page 142

Check that the letters are traced and written reasonably well.

page 143

Check that the letters are traced and written reasonably well.

page 144

Check that each letter is completed to match the letter on the left.

page 145

page 146

t: cat

n: hen

p: cap

w: cow

g: dog

page 148

Check that the numbers are traced and written reasonably well.

page 149

page 150

Check that the correct objects are drawn in the given amounts.

page 151

9 + 0 = 9

0 + 4 = 4

5 + 0 = 5

1 + 5 = 6

7 + 1 = 8

3 + 2 = 5

page 152

Check that all four objects are drawn on the map.

page 153

Check that drawings represent things that can either be seen, heard, smelled, tasted, or touched.

page 154

Check to make sure the patterns on the hats and mittens are matched correctly.

page 155

Check that each part of the picture is colored according to the key.

Skills and Standards in This Book

Today's standards have created more consistency in how mathematics and English language arts are taught. In the past, states and school districts had their own standards for each grade level. However, what was taught at a specific grade in one location may have been taught at a different grade in another location. This made it difficult when students moved.

Today, many states and school districts have adopted new standards. This means that for the first time, there is greater consistency in what is being taught at each grade level, with the ultimate goal of getting students ready to be successful in college and in their careers.

Standards Features

The overall goal for the standards is to better prepare students for life. Today's standards have several key features:

- They describe what students should know and be able to do at each grade level.
- They are rigorous and dive deeply into the content.
- They require higher-level thinking and analysis.
- They require students to explain and justify answers.
- They are aimed at making sure students are prepared for college and/or their future careers.

Unit Outline

This book is designed to help your child be prepared to meet today's rigorous standards. This section describes the standards-based skills covered in each unit of study.

Unit 1	• Prepare to write letters. • Practice letter sounds. • Draw a story and label it. • Practice writing the number 1. • Learn about circles.	• Count to three. • Compare sizes. • Observe things in a neighborhood. • Think about the weather. • Identify things that are red.
Unit 2	• Practice writing *A*, *B*, and *C*. • Practice recognizing lowercase letters. • Practice letter sounds. • Draw a story and label it. • Practice writing the number 2. • Learn about squares.	• Count to two. • Compare sizes. • Think about community helpers. • Match baby animals with their parents. • Identify things that are blue.
Unit 3	• Practice writing *D*, *E*, and *F*. • Practice recognizing uppercase letters. • Practice letter sounds. • Draw a story and label it. • Practice writing the number 3. • Learn about triangles.	• Count to three. • Compare sizes. • Think about school tools. • Identify hot and cold objects. • Identify things that are yellow.
Unit 4	• Practice writing *G*, *H*, and *I*. • Match uppercase letters with lowercase letters. • Recognize beginning sounds. • Draw a story and label it. • Practice writing the number 4.	• Learn about rectangles. • Draw up to four shapes. • Compare sizes. • Draw an adult at work. • Identify summer and winter objects. • Identify things that are green.
Unit 5	• Practice writing *J*, *K*, and *L*. • Match uppercase letters with lowercase letters. • Recognize beginning sounds. • Draw a story and label it. • Practice writing the number 5. • Identify triangles, rectangles, and circles.	• Draw up to five shapes. • Count up to five coins. • Identify objects at home that begin with *J*, *K*, and *L*. • Identify animal homes. • Identify things that are orange.

Unit 6	• Practice writing *M*, *N*, and *O*. • Recognize the letters *M*, *N*, and *O*. • Recognize beginning sounds. • Draw a story and label it. • Practice writing the number 6. • Identify triangles, squares, and circles.	• Draw up to six shapes. • Identify equal groups of coins. • Identify rules at home. • Draw pictures to show two seasons. • Identify things that are purple.
Unit 7	• Practice writing *P*, *Q*, and *R*. • Recognize the letters *P*, *Q*, and *R*. • Recognize beginning sounds. • Draw a story and label it. • Practice writing the number 7. • Trace shapes and color them in a pattern.	• Count up to seven objects. • Add objects. • Write and draw about helping others. • Put steps in order. • Identify colors.
Unit 8	• Practice writing *S*, *T*, and *U*. • Recognize the letters *S*, *T*, and *U*. • Identify rhyming sounds. • Draw a story and label it. • Practice writing the number 8. • Identify matching shapes.	• Count up to eight objects. • Add objects. • Identify where objects belong. • Identify objects that are used in different types of weather. • Color two pictures exactly the same.
Unit 9	• Practice writing *V*, *W*, and *X*. • Recognize the letters *V*, *W*, and *X*. • Identify rhyming sounds. • Draw a story and label it. • Practice writing the number 9. • Identify and color shapes.	• Draw up to nine objects. • Add objects. • Identify where different vehicles are found. • Put steps in order. • Color sets of shapes.
Unit 10	• Practice writing *Y*, *Z*, and the alphabet. • Complete partial letters. • Find hidden letters. • Recognize ending sounds. • Draw a story and label it. • Practice writing the number 0. • Identify and color shapes.	• Draw up to 10 shapes. • Add objects. • Draw places on a map. • Identify things that can be observed with the five senses. • Color a picture according to a key.

Certificate of Achievement
Congratulations
!
(name)
You have completed
Conquering Pre-Kindergarten!
presented on
(date)
Way to be a super scholar!